Golden Years
of
HALIFAX

TRUE NORTH BOOKS
DEAN CLOUGH
HALIFAX
WEST YORKS
HX3 5AX
TEL. 01422 344344
WWW.NOSTALGIA-BOOKS.CO.UK

This book is published in association with:

Calderdale College
Halifax New College
Halifax School of Integrated Arts

Golden Years of Halifax

Text........Diane Harpwood

Cover design........Mark Smith

Photographs compiled by........Phil Holland

Text pages design........Mandy Walker

Business development.........Gareth Martin

First published in Great Britain by:
True North Books, Dean Clough, Halifax HX3 5AX
1998

ISBN 1 900 463 62 8

© Copyright: True North Books

Contents

Acknowledgments

Pam & Mike Barnes (Archivist RHI), Mrs Jean Cox, Mrs Jean Emsley, Mr David Fisher (History of Local Pubs), Mr Scott Flaving DWR, Mr Stephen Gee, Mr David Greatorex (President Mytholmroyd Historical Society), Mr John Greaves, Halifax Central Library, Mr Bert Halliday, Mr Andrew Hardcastle (Historian Halifax Blue Sox), Major Harrop DWR, Mr Raymond Lawless, Mr William Norman DWR, Mr Owen Sellers, Philip S Ryley & Company, Mrs Irene Tordoff, Mr Jack Uttley, Mr Geoff Whippey, Mr John Medcalf, The Granby Public House.

Introduction

Producing another book of nostalgic reflections on the *Halifax* we used to know was a challenge taken up enthusiastically by everyone working at our small company. Over a three-year period we have produced around sixty different titles with a nostalgic theme covering most northern towns, and we consider ourselves fortunate to be able to make our living doing something so rewarding. Being dyed-in-the-wool nostalgia buffs means that we enjoy researching and writing all the titles we publish, but there is nothing that comes close to the pleasure we derive from working on books about our home town. Many people have had a hand in the preparation of *Golden Years of Halifax* ranging from the contributors who loaned photographs from their collections to a substantial group of unsung heroes who provided in-depth background information for the accompanying captions. All the people concerned have two things in common: a passion for everything associated with 'nostalgic' Halifax and a spirit of generosity which gives them pleasure from sharing their knowledge and photographs with other enthusiasts. Most of the pictures within this new collection have not been seen in book form before. We feel proud to have played our part in bringing them to the attention of a wider audience, sure in the knowledge that they will be appreciated by *Halifax lovers* everywhere.

Phil Holland
True North Books

The bottom of George Square looking from Commercial Street towards Waterhouse Street is the content of this photograph from the late 1950s. Lileys famous pram and toy shop can be seen to the right of centre in this shot and what a familiar sight this white painted establishment was to Halifax folk. Readers may recall the old treadle machines which needed good co-ordination! The treadle, underneath the machine, was operated by the foot whilst the hand span a wheel to keep the machine moving. At the same time the operator guided the fabric accurately under the 'foot', the small metal plates which held the fabric in place whilst it was being stitched. Singer was the well known manufacturer and continued to be so when treadle machines were replaced by smaller, electric machines which could handle buttonholes and embroidery! Treadle machines became popular items of furniture and have been converted into occasional and display tables the ironwork underneath the table top being an attractive feature. The Yorkshire Bank can be seen to the left of centre of this photograph and a Halifax Corporation 'bus is turning to head down Commercial Street. Is it the number 29?

Around the town centre

Below: It seems like only yesterday that deliciously hot fish and chip suppers, wrapped in last week's Evening Courier, could be had for less than a shilling. Strolling slowly home from the pub, the park or the travelling fair with our mates or our loved-one could be sheer bliss, always taking care with the stiff newspaper wrapping to keep the contents in the packet and not on the pavement. Victoria Fisheries was typical of the scores of chippies serving the suburbs of Halifax with wholesome carefully prepared hot food at prices most could run to. This is, of course, Gibbet Street in the 1940s, the picture being taken looking in the direction of Queens Road. At the junction of Queens Road and Gibbet Street, Frank Swires the chemist looked after the pharmaceutical needs of people living around and about. And at the time of writing the shop is still going strong.

Right: It is difficult to reconcile this photograph with the Cow Green we know today. This shot taken from the Bull Green end is looking in the direction of Broad Street and Crossfields, the old 'bus station. Most of this area is now filled with a multi-storey car park and the town ends of Gibbet Street, Lister and Pellon Lanes have been 'lost' in a complex of traffic lights and traffic lanes.

On the left hand side of this shot, the timbered building, is Watson's the Ironmongers who now trade from Pellon Lane. Next door is the Kings Head, a Ramsden's house which stood in this spot from 1822 until 1968. Adjacent to the Kings Head was a locksmith and the large building next along the street was a newspaper wholesalers. Further along stands Sutcliffe's curtain shop and at the end of the line of shops, left of the picture stands the Grand Junction Hotel, once a landmark in the town. Gibbet Street ran on the left of the Grand Junction and Pellon Lane on its right. The Grand Junction Hotel is shown here blackened with soot which is how many readers will remember it before its demolition, with the big golden letters spelling out its name.

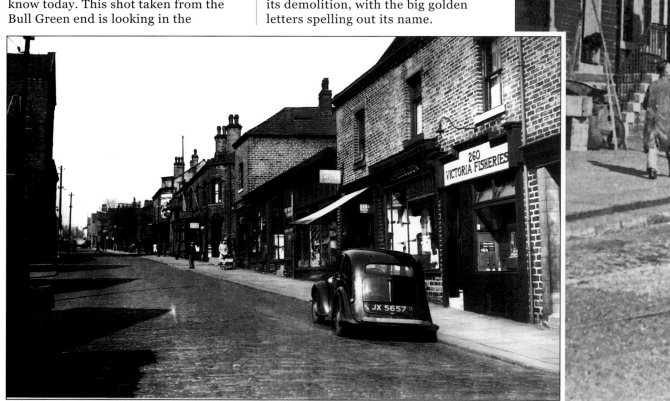

A shot taken from Commercial Street in the 1950s looking down towards Waterhouse Street. The car on the left hand edge of the photograph is a British Leyland Standard Eight which first hit the roads in 1954. Perhaps the driver was shopping in Collingwoods the Jewellers, also left of the frame, or having a cup of coffee at the Mikado Café which used to be further along the street, the sign can be seen protruding from the wall. Collingwoods is now the Halifax Estate Agency. The splendid National & Provincial Bank building can be seen at the beginning of Waterhouse Street where it remains to this day and dry cleaning is still carried out on the premises occupied by Smiths Cleaners and Dyers on this photograph. The roads are still paved with 'sets' but the gas lamps have gone to be replaced with these tall, arching electric models.

These are the days of Liberty Bodices! Anyone who ever wore one will ponder on the use of the word 'liberty'! They were close fitting with small rubber buttons which were usually misshapen from going through the mangle. A vest was also worn. Dire implications of the effect on health of going outside without both undergarments were impressed upon children by Mums of the time as they poured Cod Liver Oil down their offsprings' throats. The vests and liberty bodices could have been washed in a cream machine, a 'top loader' with an 'agitator' to swirl the water around. In less affluent households the laundry could have done in a boiler built in to the kitchen wall, perhaps a 'posser' would have been used and a rubbing board.
Remember Lonnie Donegan? He turned rubbing boards into musical instruments and formed a 'Skiffle Group'. His old man was a dustman, or so he sang.

Above: Wards End, a part of town with a fascinating history. This shot was taken looking down towards Horton Street at the turn of the century. The buildings on the right of this photograph remain to this day. The first house on the right is labelled as a surgery. Nowadays it is a sandwich shop. Commercial Street is signed as being off to the right of this picture where we would expect to see Huddersfield Road. Can readers remember the Electric Cinema along this street? Admission was 3d and 6d, there were reduced prices for children, 2d and 3d. The cinema is now the Halifax Snooker Club. A horse can just be seen drinking from Prescott Fountain the centrepiece of this photograph. The Prescott Drinking Fountain was presented to the corporation on September 12th 1884 by Mrs Leigh of Summerville, Union Street, Halifax in memory of her mother, Mrs Prescott of the same address. Their home later became Abraham Pullman's steel stockists. The fountain was moved to King Cross in 1898 and moved again to Spring Edge in 1932. It was located across the road from the back entrance to Crossley Heath School, near the area known as 'the swings' because a childrens' playground used to exist there. It remained here until 1980.

On the left hand edge of this picture a wing of Holly House, now the Bass Charrington public house, can be seen. Holly House is one of the oldest features of Wards End and dates back to 1755. In the late 1880s Doctor John Oakley lived in the house and was so moved by the illness he saw around him, he opened his home as an eye, ear and throat hospital in 1886. His work was eventually taken over by the Royal Halifax Infirmary and he gave the remainder of the funds he had raised, £240, to the Infirmary. Holly House has accommodated the School Dental Service and the Careers Service before becoming a public house. A statue of Prince Albert on his favourite horse Nimrod used to stand at the junction of Wards End, Horton Street and Southgate, in front of Holly House. The statue is now in Sparrow Park. The name 'Wards End' is likely to have been a description of the area being at the end of a 'ward' or 'beat' for a watchman. Although Wards End is referred to 'Worlds End' in the deeds of Holly House. This would certainly have been an isolated area in 1755. A Ward Hall and its extensive gardens stood on the site of what is now the ABC cinema. The cinema was first opened as the Regal and before that had been a petrol filling station. How times change!

Below: Any resident of Sowerby Bridge will quickly recognise this picture of the town, though close examination reveals several features which few modern inhabitants could have seen. The picture is dominated by the railway line, sitting high up on the embankment and running over the top of the main road leading to Ripponden and beyond to the mill towns of Lancashire. The area of open land on the left of the photograph was the site for Sowerby Bridge's open market. The road in the foreground is Station Road. It leads to the busy little railway station which has served the town for over a century and a half. The very grey appearance of the photograph has a lot to do with the huge amounts of air pollution which cursed the town from the earliest days of its industrial development. Sprouting mill chimneys are evidence of the mills and factories which caused the problem.

Left: Few Halifax folk would instantly recognise this scene as a section of King Edward Street. This is hardly surprising, as the picture was taken almost 100 years ago, before the construction of the more modern shops which line the street today. The photographer was looking in the direction of Commercial Street when he took the picture, and the substantial building on the left is therefore the old headquarters of the Halifax Building Society.

Below left: The railway at Halifax with a DELTIC locomotive diesel to the left of the photograph. The bridge which still forms the forecourt to Halifax station can be seen running across the centre of this picture with the Parish Church clearly illustrated behind the bridge. The hillside behind the Parish Church is the Claremount area and St Thomas's Church can be seen against the skyline. The spire of St Thomas's has now been taken down.

Most of the spire of All Souls Church at Boothtown, appears in the upper left hand corner of this shot and a false impression of location is given in that the church appears to be much closer to the station than it actually is. Still looking at the left of the frame, the second building from the left, is now the Imperial Crown Hotel and the road fronting these buildings now leads to the car park which serves the new Woolshops shopping centre and the new Bus Station. The arrival of Eureka, the museum for children under 12, has drastically changed the view we see here. All of the area on this side of the bridge, from the locomotive to the road in front of the buildings, has been cleared for the building of the national museum. The building has a colourful, unique design and the area around it has been lawned with benches and play items for children. The museum building can be seen from the station platforms and from the bridge. Halifax station was built in 1885.

Bottom: 'Drink Ramsdens and your friends drink with you.' This was the sign above the entrance to one of the town's most respected breweries, a popular landmark which looked out across Wards End for many decades.

Ramsden's Stone Trough Brewery is thought to date from the 1730s and was one of the oldest of the many breweries in the district. Ramsden's were absorbed into the giant Joshua Tetley group in 1964 and the site itself was cleared in 1970 to make way for the new H.Q of the Halifax Building Society which opened in 1973. The building on the right is, at the time of writing, the home of a popular nightclub.

The building dates from 1913 and was initially known as The Picture House. Name changes followed, the establishment becoming the Gaumont and then, in 1948, the Gaumont. It had seating for 1272 people who enjoyed features here until its conversion to a bingo hall in 1960. In 1973 cinema returned with the creation of the Astra with novel twin screens. By 1982 the novelty had worn off and the Astra closed. In 1988 the building found a new use, as home to the Coliseum nightclub.

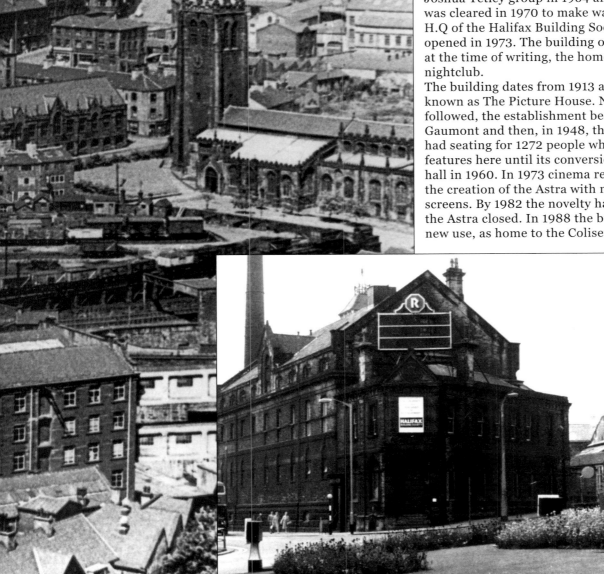

Above: Many readers may find this photograph of Bull Green in the early 1960s familiar. The number 26 Newlands 'bus is pulling away from a 'bus stop having negotiated the zebra with belisha beacons, no buttons to push or illuminated green men to watch for in this era. The parade of shops clearly visible in the picture includes Buckley and Cunliffe Shirts, the shirt makers worked above the shop, Haw and Barker, curtains, Phyllis Harper Hair Stylist, DER, television rentals and the white painted Crown and Anchor, a Whitakers public house, ends the block.
The road with its carefully laid sets and old style 'KEEP LEFT' signs is very different from today. An electric milk cart can be seen behind the central island travelling downwards towards George Square and an 'aitch' style television aerial adorns the chimney of the house top left of the photograph. People on Bull Green in November, 1959 were excited at the prospect of seeing themselves and the town on television. The famous BBC 'Tonight' programme team were in Halifax to make a short film about Wainhouse Tower. However, a newly developed drug which claimed to extend the average life to 150 years had just hit the news and the Wainhouse Tower film was shelved in favour of asking the people of Halifax their views on living to be 150. Polly Elwes was the interviewer who was 'in town that night'.

Right: Many a 'naughty but nice' cream cake has been purchased and eaten from the premises of Frank Healey, Confectioner, shown here in the 1950s. Directly around the corner was a tobacconist advertising Gold Flake cigarettes on the sign hanging from the premises. Smoking was a common practice and pleasure in those days not the subject of advertising legislation. Alec Cole, a very popular shop with the ladies, occupied the next two windows down and was a well known spot to find that special outfit. The street leads down towards Southgate, on the left the Co-op buildings can be seen, and beyond is Albion Street and the fish market.
The car in the foreground of this shot is a Hillman Californian.
The Co-op Arcade led from the spot below Alec Cole in this photograph with another entrance, or exit, on Commercial Street, which forms the present day entrance to the Co-op store. The Co-op now occupies the whole of this block ranging from the chemist, just off this shot to the left, to the travel agency, which now stands where we see Frank Healeys, and the furniture department located at the bottom on the corner adjoining Southgate. How many readers can remember wearing a navy 'gabardine' bought in the Co-op to wear to school?
The General Post Office is off to the left of this shot and the photograph has been taken from approximately where Barclays Bank stands now.

Below: The Gaiety Players were performing at the Grand Theatre in the late 1940s when this picture was taken, according to the large bill poster on the wall next to the Star Hotel. 'Vivid Whiteness' was the promise with Oxydol washing powder and the other poster promotes the consumption of Sharps Toffee. The Star Hotel remains intact, though closed as we write. The area is due to be cleared and a multi-screen entertainment centre built in its place. At the time that the photograph was taken the Odeon cinema had been in place for about a decade, and this scene was captured by the photographer standing with his back to the new facility. At the bottom of Weymouth Street a man is waiting for his lift with a suitcase and a bundle under his arm, looking hopefully in the direction of John Holdsworths, the plumber and builders merchants. The corner shop at the bottom of Weymouth Street advertises Brooke Bond Tea, Mansion Polish and Craven A cigarettes. A book could be written about the rise and fall (and some would say the rise again) of the corner shop, and the memories we all have of what proper shopping was like before the world of retailing went crackers.

Right: Bull Green and Barum Top looking down Rawson Street to the Halifax General Post Office at the bottom. Southowram Bank can be seen in the background winding up a barren Beacon Hill with familiar Halifax view of the little house against the skyline. The lower slopes of Beacon Hill are now covered in trees thanks to the efforts of volunteer tree planters. A mounted policeman can be seen in the centre of this photograph, taken in the 1950s, and over to his left a traffic island with the traditional 'Keep Left' signs. A belisha pedestrian crossing without the zebra stripes can be seen in the bottom left hand corner of this shot and the garage business behind the mounted policeman is now a kitchen appliances store. These days the placards on the right of the picture have been replaced by a multi-storey car park and Bar Centro which replaced the Comet electrical store in 1998 when Comet moved to Pellon Lane. The placards remind us that 'there's a punch in a Parsley lunch' - referring to the advertisement for Parsley salmon. Beechams Pills are also recommended by the advertiser. Bull Green is now the planned location for further parking and, in 1998, work began on the removal of the central roundabout.

Right: A nostalgic view of Bull Green, looking in the direction of Cow Green from just outside the multi-storey car park which later went on to be *Comet* and then, more recently, a trendy public house. The multi-storey car park was completed in 1966, and at the time of writing work is under way on the construction of another car park which, when completed, will dominate any modern photograph taken from this position. Many local people consider it a great shame that this well-known landmark and gateway to Halifax is being transformed almost beyond recognition.

Below: Railways and coal dominate this view, along with the more elegant lines of North Bridge, a veritable icon of Halifax and one which has graced this busy part of the town since 1872. The graceful two-spanned structure replaced a stone bridge which had served travellers for over a century. Many of the features shown in this picture have disappeared since it was taken in 1967. The Power Station and the 170 ft tall cooling towers were demolished between 1974 and 1975, the cooling towers resisting attempts to blow them up with high explosives and later being dismantled bit by bit.
Motoring features strongly in this picture, with Dews Garage's sprawling modern premises on the right of North Bridge and Cable Motors' triangular property selling Reliant three wheelers and motorbikes below it. Towards the foreground , on Old Lane underneath North Bridge, Seaman and

Davidson's the trusted expert motor engineers served a loyal clientele as they continue to do today.

Right: Much of the property in the foreground of this photograph has been cleared since it was taken in the late 1960s. Many of the present-day workers in Dean Clough would be amazed to see how many gloomy structures once lined the route to their now prestigious workplace. At one time the road leading to Illingworth was lined with squalid houses along this section and it was no loss to anyone when they were eventually cleared. On the right of this picture the cleaner lines of the Albion Court Flats can be seen towering above busy Pellon Lane. Nearer to the camera the *Cock O'the North* brewery is just one of the buildings in view, and one of many which was cleared before the new flyover was constructed in 1973. The large mill chimney in the foreground belonged to the Dean Clough Mills complex. It is long since demolished, along with some of the buildings around it, and the area is now the site of one of the centre's large car parks. This vividly illustrates how things have changed for the workers at Dean Clough over the years. It is interesting to think that in the earliest days of motoring only one or two very senior people at Dean Clough would travel to and from work by car. In modern times several hundred people use a car to get to and from their work Dean Clough, leading to several acres of parking space being created to accommodate the demand. The carpet makers from eighty years ago would be amazed by the changes.

Left: The intersection on the left of this photograph is that of North Parade and St James Road. Most of what can be seen here has since been demolished including the two cooling towers in the background, upper right of this picture, known locally as Salt and Pepper. Moving to the left and in front of the towers is Timeform, the well known Halifax racing company which still operates out of this building. In the bottom right hand corner of the photograph the foundations for the Odeon can be seen and, across the road, the Star which still stands but is scheduled for demolition. On the right hand side of the Star was once the Halifax Bowling Alley which has since been Presto and is now Netto. North Parade in the 1930s-40s held businesses and houses.

 A tobacconists, the Co-op which went through into Weymouth Street. The Co-op sold everything, clothes, furniture, wallpaper, cakes and groceries and had a Café and a function room above. Ackroyd Place School stood on the left looking down North Parade and above it stood the Baptist Church and a graveyard. A plumbers came just before St James Road and just after the junction were the premises of Rhodes a second hand shop. Above Rhodes was a pawnbroker with the traditional three balls hanging outside and, at the top, stood the Salvation Army Citadel. Looking down the right hand side of North Parade, the Co-op stood at the bottom and then private houses with steps giving onto the street continued in a terrace to the top.

Above: A view over the King Cross area taken from Warley Road, a dramatically changed part of Halifax. The clock tower of the Crossley Heath School, formerly Crossley and Porter Grammar School, can be seen poking up against the skyline. The school was built in 1863 from money donated by Sir Francis Crossley and Mr Porter. In recent years the pupils took it upon themselves to sell sponsored 'minutes' and thus raised enough money to pay for the restoration of the clock. King Cross Methodist Church, in front of the school, is still there but all the buildings between the church and the bottom of Warley Road have now been demolished in order to create a traffic light complex. Streets of terraced houses edging King Cross and the bottom of Warley Road have also been taken down and this has made space for grassy areas.

The Alan Fold public house can be seen at the right hand edge of this photograph and there used to be a police station in this vicinity.

The Halifax Fire Station is now located opposite King Cross Methodist Church on the road leading up towards Savile Park. The Fire Station used to be located on Gibbet Street and one local alderman was once honoured by having a fire engine named after him. At the naming ceremony, Alderman Fred Sharp recalled an incident when he had once almost been run down by a fire engine during his term office as Mayor of Halifax.

Below: Barum Top and the corner premises of Churchill Smith tobacconists beneath the first floor premises of the Liverpool Victoria Insurance Offices. A window facing onto Barum Top is painted over to advertise Three Castles cigarettes - Churchills was another well known brand of the time. The gentleman peering into the products displayed in the next window along could have been considering the purchase of some Barum Top Mixture, advertised along the top of the shop windows. The products which would have been sold in this shop will evoke many a memory of pipe-smoking Dads and Grandads.

Meerschaum pipes were considered the best by some and Balkan Sobranie tobacco was often a favourite with pipe smokers. It came in a round tin and had a white lid with

barrow and shovel would indicate lovers of rose growing! Workmen used to collect the horse droppings to keep the streets clean. In later years, rose growers would prize horse droppings for their gardens.

The building second from right in this picture was the Exchange Restaurant. It's name can just be seen below a first floor window.

Halifax Town Hall is a magnificent building and worthy of a book of its own. It was designed by Sir Charles Barry who also designed the Houses of Parliament, and opened in 1863 by the Prince of Wales. The opening ceremony saw Princess Street turned into a triumphal arch with a scaffolding of posts from which were draped garlands of flowers and flags for the Prince's procession to pass through.

the wording and a sketch depicted in black. Pipe smoking was always associated with the qualities of steadiness and calmness, you could always rely on a pipe smoker! They carried their tobacco in pouches often made of soft leather and had small, cylindrical 'tampers' to pack the tobacco tightly into the bowl of the pipe. The stem could be removed for cleaning and the habit afforded lots of ideas for gifts for the 'man who had everything'. How things have changed. Imagine the furore if someone lit a pipe in a restaurant or office nowadays - although the aroma was enjoyed by some it was pungent and unmistakable. George Street, as it was, leads down to the left of the picture and a Morris Minor can be seen speeding away on the right of this shot in the direction of Bull Green.

Right: Halifax Town Hall seen at exactly nine minutes past ten in the morning. The Town Hall clock affords total precision as to the time this photograph was taken, unfortunately the year is more difficult to establish! The horses and carriages drawn up outside the Town Hall would indicate the turn of the century and the nearby

Soldiers with rifles lined the street and mounted horseguards in plumed helmets formed part of the parade. Before the Town Hall was built, the town elders had to meet in Kershaw's Warehouse. The town office was a shabby, third storey room with a rattling printing press above and the boisterous goings-on of a third-rate beer house underneath.

The handsome stone balustrade in Highroad Well Park was once part of the east side of the Town Hall. It was removed many years ago to ease traffic congestion. The balustrade is situated beside the memorial to the Halifax men who died in the Boer War. Originally, the Town Hall housed the police station and all the council departments. The police moved to Harrison Road in 1900 and various council departments began to move out from 1890. The Town Hall's soot blackened look was cleaned away in 1972. Some Town Hall vital statistics include the fact that the intricately carved spire soars 180 feet into the sky. Its building used 24,000 tons of local sandstone from Swalesmoor Quarries, the hour bell weighs 79 cwts and there are no less than 140 ornamental stone pillars.

Below: A sunny and ceremonial Saturday afternoon in Halifax in May, 1952. This year saw Princess Elizabeth become Queen Elizabeth II, Sovereign of the United Kingdom and of the British Commonwealth and Empire, succeeding her father King George VI. A year later was the coronation and also the conquering of Everest for the first time by Sir Edmund Hillary and Sherpa Tensing who were members of Colonel John Hunt's expedition. Seven earlier attempts had failed, some with loss of life.

This photograph taken, at the bottom of George Square looking down Commercial Street, shows the Territorial Army Band under the leadership of Bandmaster F Ashton-Jones. The band formed part of the 250th anniversary parade of the Duke of Wellington's Regiment which marked the beginning of two days of celebrations. The huge crowds which turned out for the event can be seen on the photograph with one man climbing onto the roof of Gledhill Hosier, right hand side of the picture. The stack of the old Odeon cinema can be seen in the distance, centre right, and the Yorkshire Penny Bank building is in front. The parade of shops on the right of the shot included Asquith's umbrella and handbag shop, and Ainley's tobacconist who sported a sign advertising State Express 555 cigarettes. Cheapside meets Commercial Street at around this point and readers may remember Lileys pram and toy shop which occupied the corner plot for many years. The site is now used by Klick Photopoint and Specsavers. Marks and Spencers were associated with Cheapside until their move in 1998.

Right: When is a street not a street? When it's a square! The confusion as to whether George Square is George Square or George Street arose because, once upon a time, there were both. George Street and old properties in George Square were pulled down in 1938 and then began a dream, a plan, an architect's project under construction which resulted in the George Square we know today. The project was finally completed in 1959. In the photograph the telephone booths, right of centre, will stir memories for many a reader. In this period, late 1950s - early 1960s, these booths were rather trendy and stylishly modern - cool even! Stoddarts fabric shop can be seen on the right of the shot, beneath the Anglo American Chewing Gum sign, with Masons, menswear, next door. The position of the 'bus in this picture shows the two-way nature of traffic at this time - the number 35 Highroad Well used to run from George Square. The new block, upper left of centre, housed the well known hairdresser Irvine Lodge - a real treat to have a hairdo from this establishment. Hagenbach's confectionery shop was, at one time, below Irvine Lodges. These premises are now occupied by Whitegates Estate Agency, Kentucky Fried Chicken and Just Jenna, bridal wear. George Square could have been named after Loveledge Lane which once stood on this site, but it wasn't. It could have been named Somerset Street after the magnificent Somerset House, a hidden treasure of the town standing above and behind the present day Yorkshire Building Society. The front of Somerset House can also be seen behind the shops on Rawson Street. However, it wasn't. George Square was named after a king of Denmark who once stayed as a guest at Somerset House.

Sporting life

Above: Mr Raymond Lawless, a resident still of Luddenden Foot, can be seen second from right on the front row of this photograph, seated with arms folded next to the man in the suit and behind the cup. Mr Lawless played centre forward on the winning team pictured and will celebrate his 90th birthday in November. There's likely to be a party at Luddenden Foot Bowling Club! The team changed into their kit in the old Boys Brigade building which is now the Brandy Wine public house on the bridge in Luddenden Foot.

The photograph is believed to have been taken on the old football ground which is still there and rented out by the local authority to various users. The team had a pie supper at the Black Lion on the road towards Halifax to celebrate their win and the club President, Mr Harry Helliwell, footed the bill. The best goal Mr Lawless ever scored was from a pass from the man on his right looking at the photograph, Mr Buckley. Sadly, most of the men on this picture are no longer with us, some were lost in the Second World War.

Mr Lawless has been a member of Luddenden Foot Bowling Club for 65 years and has held the positions of President, groundsman and barman. The club in its most attractive, riverside surroundings, opened in 1913.

Right: Halifax Rugby League Team, captained by Harry Beverley, beat Salford in the 1939 Cup Final and returned home to a rapturous welcome and an estimated 100,000 turned out to meet and greet the victorious team. The crowds were thickest around the railway station where selected officials and members of the town council had gathered to meet and congratulate the team. Barriers were used to hold back the huge crowd eager to see the players and to prevent them from overwhelming the reception party and area. Some more enterprising supporters simply travelled to Sowerby Bridge and bought a ticket to Halifax. They arrived at the appropriate platform at the appropriate time and the numbers in the reception party swelled somewhat! The team and reception party travelled in a cavalcade of motor coaches to the Town Hall where this photograph was taken and where the people of Halifax traditionally welcome their cup winners. This photograph, taken on May 8th 1939, is also an excellent illustration of the old style police uniform, these are the days of the bobby on the beat and the bicycle. As can be seen, the supporters include rosette wearing women and children as well as men, this mixed support seems to be a feature of rugby league. This stunning picture was discovered, along with other rugby memorabilia, by staff at The Granby Public House at Gibbet Street during decorating and very kindly loaned to us for this book.

Right: Eleven proud lads, a twelfth man and two teachers in this photograph which shows us Siddal School's winning cricket team taken during the war. On the left of this picture is Mr Bert Halliday in his younger days who donated this picture. Behind him is Mr Allan who was the Headmaster at that time, the other teacher, right of this shot, was Mr Dooley the sports teacher.

Siddal Board School was founded in July 1875 and Siddal County Junior School, which it has become, held a concert in July, 1975 to commemorate its centenary. Parrot fashion learning was in vogue in 1875 and, a century later having looked into school records, the children of 1975 recited a very moral poem to illustrate the differences in approaches to learning including how pupils used to be tested in readiness for the visits by the Schools Inspector - enough to strike terror into the heart of any schoolboy or girl! The 20th century children performed in choirs and played musical instruments including violins, recorders and percussion instruments. They put on a display of work illustrating school life as it had been 100 years earlier and more than 50 of the girls modelled clothes they had made during the school year. Mr I Smith, the Headteacher in 1975, had wanted to stage an event relevant to the occasion and he thanked the staff and the children for their efforts in doing just that.

Below: The excitement, the thrills and spills of rugby league. Thrum Hall take on Workington in this photograph in the famous blue and white striped shirts. The team of the 1950s was one of Halifax's all time great sides although we weren't too successful in the Cup Finals of the period, more often runners-up, we lost once, drew once and then lost the replay. The quality of the team in the 50s is put down to the fact that players stayed with the club for long periods, as long as ten years, and also, we had a ferocious pack! The names of Jack Wilkinson, Alvin Ackerly, John Henderson and Albert Fearnley were enough to strike terror into the hearts of many an opponent. Dean and Kielty as half-backs prospered from the efforts of the forwards and with Johnny Freeman and Arthur Daniels on the wings Halifax was a force to be reckoned with!

A book on the history of Thrum Hall, 'The Thrum Hall Story', by Andrew Hardcastle was published in 1986. Andrew Hardcastle had a second book published in 1994, 'Thrum Hall Greats', which gives the stories of the players honoured with a place in the Hall of Fame set up in 1993.

March 21st 1998 saw the final first team game to be held at Thrum Hall when Halifax played at home to Leeds Rhinos. To mark the event there was a procession of past players and the players of tomorrow, featuring local junior clubs. An under-15s game was played between Elland Boxers and Sowerby Bridge Robins and half-time community singing was led by Scott Conrad and the Todmorden Old Brass Band. At the end of it all the announcer, in vain, asked the crowds to please keep off the pitch. Hundreds of people, of course, ignored the plea and spent a few minutes lingering on the park to take away their final memory of Thrum Hall.

Below: A schoolboy reaches out to touch his hero and the crowd throng the park at Thrum Hall after a Halifax win. Arthur Daniels, the well known player seen in this shot, had scored four tries in this game. Daniels played 376 games for Halifax and scored a total of 215 tries. He also successfully kicked two goals. Signed by the club in 1945 he played until the 1956-57 season when he retired and a testimonial game was played.

Daniels was an ex- rugby union man, a former Welsh International who had played for Llanelli RUFC. He was a winger, a fearless player who has earned his place in the Hall of Fame set up at Thrum Hall in 1993. Andrew Hardcastle, the club historian, has published two books, 'The Thrum Hall Story' and 'Thrum Hall Greats'. The first tells the history of the club and the second the stories of the players honoured with a place in the Hall of Fame.

Supporters have travelled to Wembley to watch Halifax play in cup finals on several occasions. The whole town has turned out to mob the Town Hall to see them return with the cup on three occasions - 1931, 1939 and 1987. Halifax, of course, has won the cup on more than three occasions, the other wins pre-date the using of Wembley stadium as the cup final venue. Prior to Wembley the Cup Final was held on various club grounds including Headingly and Odsal.

People, although sad to see the end of Thrum Hall for first team games, have accepted the move to the Shay. The Thrum Hall stadium was over 100 years old and it is hoped that at the Shay sharing with Halifax Town FC, two lots of funding will be drawn into the stadium.

At leisure

Right: Taken from the top of the Town Hall, this photograph gives a rare view of the early stages of the construction of the Odeon Cinema. It was taken in 1937 and the steel framework for the building has almost been completed. Land behind the Odeon would later become the site of the Cross Field bus station and later still the home of the local D.S.S offices. The Odeon opened for business on June 27th 1937 with seating for 2,055. The cinema closed in October 1975 but opened two years later as the Top Rank Bingo club.

Interestingly, another fine local servant in the field of entertainment can be seen in the distance on St.James Road. The Alhambra was built in 1840 and stood on St. James Road until it was pulled down in 1963. Readers may remember the establishment as the Halifax Friendly and Trades Club. Its days as a cinema spanned a period between 1917 and 1959. Charles Dickens and Franz Liszt both performed there.

Facing page, bottom left: As victorian Halifax grew and civic pride grew with it, it was felt that the town needed a symbol of that pride, a crowning glory almost. The Victoria Hall, seen in this photograph, was built to be that symbol of civic pride. A prime location was chosen, the junction of Commercial Street and Fountain Street and the Victoria Hall with its distinctive twin towers was built in 1900 and opened in February, 1901. The floor was designed and built on special springs which was the modern equivalent of 'state of the art' in those days. The quality of this floor was the subject of much complimentary comment and pride. The evening of February 8th, 1901, was the gala opening and the audience were entertained in their brand new hall by Dr Hans Richter, conductor, and a combined orchestra. The accoustics of the Hall were described as the best in England for choral singing and the Halifax Choral Society gave a performance to put that claim to the test.

In 1935 the Halifax Choral Society performed once again at the Victoria Hall. This time the world famous local tenor, Mr Walter Widdop, joined them in a performance of 'The Messiah' which was broadcast by the BBC.

The Victoria Hall eventually became the Civic Theatre and is now known as The Victoria Theatre. Halifax people still attend their Hall for a wide range of entertainments from the Northern Ballet to an annual pantomime.

This photograph is likely to date from the 1910-20 period. A tram can just be seen outside the General Post Office on the right of the picture and a horse has definitely passed through the area in the foreground!

Facing page, bottom right: This scene will stir many a Halifax memory! A rare picture of the Grand Theatre which stood on the Halifax end of North Bridge. The Grand began life as a hotel, became a theatre and, in this picture, has become a cinema. Showing tonight was Douglas Fairbanks Jr in 'Parachute Jumper'. Many a good night out has been had at the Grand and a production of 'Face at the Window' once terrified Halifax audiences.

Eric Portman the Halifax actor who achieved fame and fortune in Hollywood, appeared at the Grand in Arsenic and Old Lace. His leading lady was Beatrix Leaman who also went to Hollywood. The Charles Denville Theatre Company put on the plays and several of their actors became well known. John Wentworth is one who went into films. The D'Oyly Carte Opera company has also performed at the Grand.

The Globe Hotel, to the right of the Grand, will also stir a few thoughts. Note the old telephone box at the left of this shot.

North Bridge which leads off towards Boothtown from the left of this picture, was opened in 1872. The present two span iron bridge replacing the former old stone bridge which dated back to the 18th century.

Below: A lovely view of the beautiful Peoples Park in bloom on a weekend or holiday. In the background can be seen the magnificent building which was once Belle Vue Library and is now the head offices of a local company. Peoples Park is located just below Francis Street and Calderdale College and stretches between King Cross Road and Hopwood Lane. The people seated on the benches in this shot are on the terrace, slightly higher than and overlooking the parkland, the fountain and the bandstand. At the bottom of the park could be found a meandering 'river' with swans and rocks and bushes planted to give a natural appearance. Children could hide and run under the bridge, feed the swans with breadcrumbs and paddle in the pond surrounding the fountain.

A beautiful park indeed and given to the people of Halifax by Sir Francis Crossley in August 1857 when 10 bands and thousands of people thronged the park to celebrate the opening. The park is said to have cost £30,000 with an additional endowment of £6,300 for its upkeep. Designed by Sir Joseph Paxton who also designed the Crystal Palace, the park was accepted on behalf of the people by the Mayor of Halifax, John Whitworth. A few years later a statue of Sir Francis Crossley was erected in the park.

Right: This thought-provoking photograph was taken in the 1920s. The occasion was the funeral of the Reverend Father Bradley, the much loved and respected Parish Priest at St. Bernards Roman Catholic Church. This is a small section of the 5000-strong party of mourners who had turned out to pay their last respects. All but three of the boys are wearing caps and armbands - complete with sombre crosses as a mark of respect on the sad day.

Top hats were the height of respect for the male adults in the photograph, along with smartly cut coats and crisp, white winged collars. The lady on the right of the scene looks entirely in keeping with our perception of 1920s-style clothing for well dressed middle-aged women. It was said that the whole of Halifax came to a stand-still for the funeral of this popular priest. No doubt these stern adults would have ensured that the children in their charge would all have been on their best behaviour.

A local College for local people

As we move towards the year 2000 Calderdale Colleges Corporation celebrates over a century of educational achievement and service to the local community. Although the College Corporation has grown rapidly and changed dramatically during its one hundred years there are strong elements of continuity in its story. These links can be most clearly seen in the College's partnerships with the local community, local business and the local authority and its enduring commitment to providing education and career opportunities for Calderdale people.

The College's roots are in the self-improvement tradition of the nineteenth century and the Victorian ideal of useful service to the community. Two of the direct lineal ancestors of the Corporation were the Halifax Mechanics Institute and the Halifax School of Art.

The Mechanics Institute was founded in 1825 to provide general education and practical classes in self-improvement for local working people in areas such as textile engineering, mathematics, shorthand and reading. The Halifax School of Art was founded in 1859 and provided 'art instruction in the useful and decorative arts for local mechanics'. By 1890 the art classes were held in the Belle Vue buildings in Hopwood Lane which had been handed over to the local council.

These evening classes continued to be popular and there was a strong demand for larger, purpose-built accommodation. Although the Mechanics Institute and the School of Art were voluntary bodies they did receive financial aid from the Halifax Borough Council and gifts and donations from private individuals and businesses.

In a way that has many striking contemporary parallels national government initiatives played an important part in the College's foundation and initial development.

From the 1870s there was a growing awareness of the need to improve education and training standards in Britain. Various royal commissions and government

Above: Alderman Percival Whitley, closely identified with the development of the College.

reports argued that Britain was falling behind her economic rivals who were investing in the new technologies and technical, vocational education. To remedy this, government initiatives such as Technical Institution Act 1889, aimed to create a system of technical education and expand education opportunities beyond the elementary school leaving age of eleven. Britain's continuing economic success, it was believed, would depend in the future on an educated and well-qualified workforce.

Something of how this national mood was reflected locally could be seen in the debates about the foundation of the College and the minute books of the council committee that controlled the College. One of the local supporters of this movement in this early period was Alderman J.W Davies who saw direct economic and cultural benefits for local people in the development of the College. At the laying of the Foundation Stone on May 23rd 1893 he put the College's role into a wider (and very modern) context:

'Industries are in a constant state of transition owing to new discoveries and new initiatives, and we need people who can take advantage of all the changes which our industries are undergoing and who have the necessary flexibility and elasticity of mind to grasp these opportunities.'

From the very beginning the modern College has been a partnership with local employers and community organisations playing a prominent role on the governing body and influencing the curriculum. Local companies and benefactors subscribed to the original funds and provided teaching equipment for the College: the Halifax Incorporated Chamber of Commerce contributed to the development of the commercial Education scheme, set examinations and offered prizes to successful students in the 1890s.

By modern standards the College was small. Based in Hopwood Lane when classes began in 1896 it consisted of one laboratory, a weaving shed and various classrooms; the staff consisted of one full-time teacher and twenty three part-time staff who taught 1,000 students.

The teaching curriculum was influenced by the major industries and interests of Calderdale's communities. The College had departments of textiles, engineering, chemistry, commerce and women's work. The early records and prospectuses give a real flavour of its every day, or rather every evening, life.

We read of courses in dye-making, plumbing, textile design and university extension lectures in English history. The registers show how local individuals used the College to develop new skills and gain qualifications; we see waiters learning commercial and catering French, clerks in local mills studying book-keeping and short-hand and elementary teachers studying for University of London external degrees.

As an essential part of the community the College shared in all the major successes and challenges faced by Calderdale people. Members of staff and students fought in the two world wars and the College made a contribution to the war effort between 1939-45 by training engineering workers for vital war work, teaching food supply and organisation for the Ministry of War and running courses in army organisation for

the ATS. At the conclusion of both wars the College was involved with rehabilitation and retraining programmes for demobilised service personnel.

The College archives contain a discharged soldiers and sailors record book that reveals how the College helped the soldiers injured and scarred by the traumas of the Western Front recover and build a new life in the post-war world after 1918. The bald statistics and records of course organisation also contain individual stories of how education and training could make a real difference to the lives of local people.

As well as the obvious training programmes for service and war production personnel the College also made an unusual contribution to the war effort. In 1942 the Army Education Corps organised 'schemes of recreational occupation for men and women in isolated camps.' Groups of sergeant instructors from the Army and the ATS were trained in bookbinding and soft toy making at the College's School of Art and sent back to

Below: A meeting of Principals in West Yorkshire.

Mr J Crowther (first Principal 1895 - 1930) with his staff.

An early sporting achievement

their various camps to give similar training to service personnel.

The Second World War interrupted pre-war plans to extend the College. These had reached an advanced stage at the outbreak of war in 1939: when these plans were reconsidered in the 1950s they were revised to take account of the changing needs of College students.

Drawn up by the local architects Pickles & Son the new multi storied building aimed to centralise all the activities of the College in one building. The School of Art and women's departments were transferred from the Queens Road buildings to the new centre. Designed to incorporate the latest design features and teaching facilities the new building on Francis Street was a visible embodiment of the local pride and sense of municipal achievement Halifax people felt for their College.

As well as a new building the College also got a new name which reflected the changing nature of its work. In September 1957 when the Francis Street building opened the old Halifax Municipal Technical College was renamed the Percival Whitley College of Further Education.

This new title was significant for two reasons. Firstly the name commemorated the work of Alderman Percival Whitley, a former mayor of Halifax and Chairman of the Halifax Education Committee for thirty years who also was closely identified with the development of education in the borough and with the growth of the College in particular. Percival Whitley exemplified the strengths of the West Riding non-Conformist and Liberal tradition with its commitment to education and public service. His educational vision was a broad one, seeing education in a wider context that linked the academic, the vocational and the recreative functions of the College. It was a vision that was to have a clear influence on the College as it grew in the 1950s and 1960s.

Secondly the addition of the title 'Further Education' represented a qualitative change in the activities and role of the College. As in the 1890s national developments in education and social policy had an impact locally. The 1944 Education Act raised issues of the reorganisation of secondary education whilst successive post-war governments saw education playing a vital role in the rebuilding of Britain after the Second World War. 'Further Education' was a new concept in post-

compulsory education. It had a broader function than simply technical and vocational education, allowing individuals a chance to realise their potential and gain new qualifications or develop new interests. In these idealistic terms further education had a key role in the

Above: Looking to the future - students from the women's department in the 1940s.

new opportunities provided by the Welfare State Britain of the 1950s.

The Percival Whitley College prospectus reflected this broader view: whilst many of the standard course subjects had remained unchanged for much of the twentieth century, new 'A' level, 'O' level and interest based programmes began to appear in areas such as cookery, literary appreciation and languages. A 1957 Halifax Courier article described a College Open Day in the following terms: 'There was something for everyone of the thousands of people who attended the College Open Day... It's the College where all ages go' and '... its students gain one of the finest education available in the country.' This was reflected in the accompanying picture, which showed local women listening to radio transmissions from the recently launched Soviet Sputnik Satellite, which was beamed directly into the College.

Despite the changes most of the College's students in the 1950s and 1960s were part-time or on day release courses. The majority of these students were following work-related programmes which reflected the nature of the local economy and continuing domination of Calderdale's traditional industries. During this period there can have been few people in local companies who did not have some links with the College, either as former students of the College themselves or by sending employees as students.

But, as the Halifax Courier report quoted above indicates, the College acted as a focal centre for local life providing a venue for student and community activity ranging from amateur dramatics and social events through to charity fund raising and College societies such as the Scientific Society and the Outdoor Pursuits Group. The annual reports of the College principal and the cutting books of local newspapers detail an active, vibrant learning community that played a real role in expanding the horizons and the potential of the local community. Every year shows successful students collecting examination certificates, smiling groups of adults in an evening class or local school children

visiting the College to use its facilities; these snapshots over a thirty-year period give a real flavour of the developing life of the College.

The pace of change accelerated rapidly in the 1970s and 1980s reflecting wider changes in the local economy, local government reorganisation and national government policies. In particular, the relative decline of traditional industries, increasing student expectations and a desire for educational opportunity and an increased central government emphasis on education as a crucial component of national economic success and social policy had significant impact on the College.

The annual reports, prospectuses and press cuttings of these years tell a story of an institution that is evolving and developing in line with the community around it. Although many curriculum areas would have been familiar to the Victorian founders of the College the impact of 'new technology' and changing patterns in the world of work had major effects on the College. During the 1970s and 1980s there was a clear shift towards increasing numbers of full-time students including new groups of adults who saw the College as offering a 'second chance' and younger 16-19 year olds to whom the College represented a real alternative to school in an era of increased participation in education for young people over 16 years of age.

The College curriculum in these years showed elements of both continuity and discontinuity. Building on its tradition of responding to local business needs and economic change the College was locally in the forefront

Below: A view of Halifax New College - the area's sixth form College.

D Floor Computing in 1985.

of introducing new technology in the late 1960s and 1970s. As early as 1969 the College was organising short courses for local companies in areas as diverse as 'metrication for plumbers,' Cobol and Fortran programming, and electronics. But the changing fortunes of the textile department were a sign of the times. From being a mainstay of the Victorian College textiles had only one permanent teacher by 1969; a staff report reflected the discussion about falling interest in the industry; it was agreed that 'young people did not see any future in the industry and that the raising of the school leaving age had affected recruitment.'

The 1980s probably saw the most radical change in the College's history. The patterns of change continued with a shift from areas such as engineering and day-release programmes to courses related to the new service industries that was becoming such a key part of the local economy. Word processing, tourism and leisure, hospitality and catering and business administration were expanding areas along with access programmes for adults which offered alternative routes to higher education and careers.

Government policy contributed to these radical changes. The College worked closely with the Manpower Services Commission, the Training and Enterprise Councils and agencies of the European Community to develop programmes for retraining and upskilling local

people as the economy was restructured. In 1988 the College's name was changed from Percival Whitley College of Further Education to Calderdale College reflecting local government reorganisation and the changing nature of the College's activities. The memory of Percival Whitley was kept alive by the name of the main College building and the annual Percival Whitley lecture, which gave prominent people an opportunity to share their vision of education to a wider audience.

The Education Reform Act (1988) and the Further and Higher Education Act (1992) marked the single most dramatic change in the College organisation since the 1890s. This incorporated further education Colleges as organisations separate from local authority control; supervision now passed to the Department of Education with financial and other functions carried out by a government agency, the Further Education Funding Council. In effect the College passed from local authority to central government control.

However as the College evolved during the 1990s it retained close links with the local community: the new governing body of the incorporated College was initially drawn from the local business community and it's membership has been broadened to include local authority representatives and other community representation.

A further renaming of the institution occurred in 1997 when Calderdale Colleges Corporation was established. This umbrella title was created to oversee the brands of; Calderdale College (further and higher education), Halifax School of Integrated Arts (arts, design, performance, construction and horticulture), Halifax New College (the sixth form College specialising in A levels and Advanced G.N.V.Q.), Local Learning (community-based adult education delivered in 50 local centres throughout the area), Calderdale Associates Ltd (the company which contract with Training and Enterprise Councils to provide training) and Calderdale Catering Ltd (the company which provides hospitality and catering training).

With a budget of over £12million and contacts with over 240 companies and organisations throughout the area Calderdale Colleges Corporation is now a major education and training organisation.

As the College Corporation looks forward to its next century it is keen to build on the strengths and traditions of the past one hundred years. Training and education of high quality are going to be even more important in the future development of Britain's economy.

At the 1993 Percival Whitley Lecture, Howard Davies, Director General of the C.B.I argued that if Britain's economy was to be 'fit for the future and competitive on a world scale our training and education has to be of world class.'

Just as our Victorian forebears recognised the value of quality education and training to enable local companies and workers to meet the challenges of a new century so Calderdale Colleges Corporation sees itself as central to the development of individuals, companies and communities of Calderdale in the years ahead.

Percival Whitley College, Francis Street in 1988.

On the move

Facing page, bottom right: It is 1928 and no-one has heard of driving tests and MOTs. The growth of motor transport and increases in the number of vehicles on the road, tramlines, slippery surfaces and cobbles all conspired to raise the number of accidents. A crowd of onlookers has gathered here after a motor-bike and side-car has come a cropper on a bend in the road at Luddenden Foot. After buying a motor-bike, often a Panther, a side-car could be purchased to carry passengers. Side-cars were bolted on and could be removed if wished. They never appeared to be comfortable vehicles and were low, close to the road.

The name of Luddenden Foot means the valley of the River Lud where it joins the Calder.

As can be seen on the right of this photograph, gas street lighting was installed and operational in Luddenden Foot in the 1920s. It had, in fact, arrived in the area a little over 60 years earlier on December 4th, 1866. Much pomp and circumstance surrounded its arrival and the Luddenden Foot Band paraded through the village.

A celebratory supper was held for the management committee and subscribers at the Anchor and Shuttle Inn following the official lighting of the lamps. The subscribers to the scheme had done so to 'add much to the comfort of pedestrians and be preventative to future accidents'.

Facing page, bottom left: 'Oh no,' is possibly what the little boy to the right of this photograph is saying! The car, an Austin Six and belonging to the Mayor of Halifax, has probably had a bump in the blackout. Wartime blackout shades cover the head-lamps and a crumpled AA badge lies with the innards of the broken headlight somewhere near to the badly bent front bumper! All streets and build-ings had to be 'blacked out' and this was an outdoor world completely devoid of artificial light in order to foil the navigational efforts of enemy aircraft and 'spotter' 'planes.

Halifax homes had to be equipped with 'blackout' curtains which were generally made as linings sewn into the family's usual curtains.

Housewives bought a dull, satin-like, black fabric specially produced for this purpose with which to make their blackout curtains. Some households had thin wooden boards made to fit their windows exactly and factories had to paint their windows. Social events tend to take place indoors after dark, the problem was getting to them during the black-out! Cinemas remained open during the war and the radio was a popular source of entertainment - Vera Lynn and Dick Barton Special Agent numbered amongst the popular programmes of the era. Name boards were removed from railway stations and other places which could assist the enemy to iden-tify their whereabouts. You had to know where you were going in those days! At the end of the blackout there was much celebration and the top of Wainhouse Tower was illuminated to commem-orate the event.

Right: 'Oops' is perhaps the appropriate word to accompany this picture! Is this an early 'ram-raid' or a dreadful acci-dent?. The latter seems to be the most likely. It appears that the car, a Standard or possibly a foreign car, has hit the shop front with consid-erable force, possibly dislodging what could be a shop sign which has landed on top of the car. The smart lady passing by, to the right of the photograph, is smiling which might indicate that no-one was injured in this accident despite the damage to the front of the car. A police offi-cer and another man can just be seen on the far side of the crashed vehi-cle. This photograph was taken on Southgate look-ing along Cornmarket towards the Town Hall which can be seen to the right of centre in the background of the shot. Lister Horsfall's remains in this same spot, at the bottom of Cheapside, to this day. Although the modernisation of the shop front has changed its appearance, and the modern security measures are a little firmer than these crushed grills over the windows, the sign above the shop appears unchanged. Jackson the photographer had premises in this parade of shops and, moving on towards the Town Hall, was, and still is, the White Swan Hotel. The modern building which housed Burton the tailors can just be seen on the upper right edge of the photograph and above Burtons was the Empress Ballroom. This night spot is known to a later gener-ation as 'Palings' but whatever the generation, it has been the scene of many a good night out!

Above: Wonderful smells are what everyone associated with Collinsons. The 30 cwt lorry shown here dates from the 1920s and appears to be dressed for the Infirmary Procession - the pre-cursor to the Halifax Charity Gala - and boasts the fact that Collinsons have been 'Blenders of fine teas since 1835'. A map of India and Ceylon, now Sri Lanka, stands in the centre of the flatback showing the areas where the 'fine teas' were grown.

Craftsmen in Collinsons fragrant warehouse, which used to stand in St Johns place, blended, roasted or graded goods from coffee to rice, from tea to sultanas and all were experts in their trades. An exotic mix of sacks of coffee beans from Kenya and Central America, chests of tea from Java, Sumatra and China were stacked in the warehouse.

Founded by Thomas Collinson in 1835, the company stood first and last for quality and their outlets relied on their high standards. The company closed with their good name intact and a contemporary comment was 'No-one can take that away.'

Collinsons had an extremely popular Crown Street Café and shop which closed in 1962. Jowett and Sowry the stationers were later on the same site before their closure in 1998. Readers may remember the Collinson sign of gold lettering on a dark green background and many will certainly remember those wonderful cups of coffee and cream cakes!

Right: George C Pratley & Son of North Parade are advertising their wares on this well polished Commer van of the 1950s. The photograph was taken on Huddersfield Road as Trinity Garage can be seen in the background as 'Distributors of Hillman Sunbeam'. Readers will be interested in a book found in Trinity Garage in August 1998 during re-decoration of the premises. The book, a leather bound record of minutes of meetings and company reports held during the First World War, gives a fascinating insight into the thoughts of the then Board of Directors. An example would be a quote from the Chairman of the company in 1914, Mr Sam Hoyle, who said, '...that the heart of the world beats in our Metropolis and the provinces are awakening to the benefits and economies of the motor system.' Elsewhere in the book the directors stated that 'they could not see the day when their employees would be able to afford to buy a car'!

There are plans to restore the book and display it in the garage for customers to browse through.

Below: Did you know that your bird cage should have a 'Clipper' water fountain? That is the case according to the message on the back of this van. It is no great problem because the notice on the van also tells us that we can buy one from our pet store for 1/6d each. Therein could lie a problem! 1 shilling is 12 old pennies or 5 new pence! Six old pennies are equal to 2.5 new pence. There were 20 shillings and 240 old pennies in £1 whereas nowadays shillings don't exist and there are 100 new pence in £1. Threepenny bits ...... The van in the picture is a 30 cwt Commer vehicle from the 1960s, a Superpoise Super Capacity Van to be precise. Thomas's of Halifax began as a small family affair at Ambler Thorn about 1880. Their business was breeding and dealing in all varieties of canary and by 1918 trade had increased to such an extent that they bought a warehouse in Charles Street, Halifax and expanded the business to include cake bird foods, breeding cages and other pet accessories. World War II saw the company involved in the manufacture of light armaments but after the war Thomas's continued to grow adding dog equipment and aquatic pet products to their catalogue. The brand name 'Petcraft' was adopted and, at the time of their takeover by the Mars Group in 1968, Petcraft boasted that almost all budgie owners used one or more of their products. The eventual Pellon Lane factory was moved to Gomersal in 1986/7 and most of the 300 employees went too. The Pellon Lane building had previously been owned by Philips before their move to Lightcliffe.

Below: This photograph from the late 1960s gives a clear view of the building of the tunnel at Ainley Top over which the M62 would scythe its way between Hull and Liverpool. Were the drivers of these cars waiting patiently at the temporary traffic lights? History, they say, repeats itself and certainly drivers down The Ainleys from Huddersfield have experienced a great deal of waiting during 1998 due to maintenance work and the changing of road layouts. The Calder and Hebble public House stood at the entrance to the town from The Ainleys, at the junction of Wakefield Road and Salterhebble Hill, at the end of the stretch known locally as Elland Wood Bottom. Elland Wood Bottom retains its paved walkway and railings to this day although its popularity as a place for young women to meet young men on Sunday evening strolls seems to have waned! The bright lights and night-clubs of the town centre are now the draw for the young and single set. In the early days of the century the top of the rise from Elland Wood Bottom was the site of the Halifax Zoo, can any readers remember that leisure attraction? The early numbers of the present Chevinedge are said to be built on the old bear pit.

The cars queuing at the traffic lights are, from the front, an old Ford Cortina and an Austin Cambridge followed by two Morris 1100s.

> *In the early part of the century the top of the rise from Elland Wood Bottom was the site of the Halifax Zoo.*

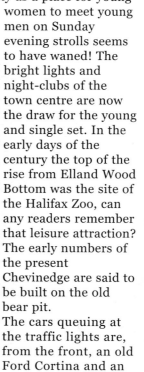

The number 30 Southowram 'bus stopping to pick up a passenger on Charlestown Road in the 1960s. Eagle eyed readers will be able to spot the Brickmakers Arms on New Bank on the left hand side of the photograph and the billboard urging us to 'Chew Wrigleys Gum' on the side of the house on the right of the picture. The 'bus is a Halifax Corporation Leyland and, happily for 'bus enthusiasts, old style 'buses have been recently re-introduced on a couple of local routes. The Halifax motor 'bus service was fully developed in the period between 1926 - 1930 but the history of 'buses in Halifax goes back a long way. In February, 1865 a meeting was held at The Old Cock Hotel to discuss the formation of 'The Halifax Omnibus Company' and, by the end of that year a 'bus was running between King Cross and Boothtown via Northgate. There were two fare stages each costing 3d for 'inside' and 2d for 'outside'. King Cross to Northgate, at the time of writing would cost around 44 new pence which would equate with 106 old pennies - confused? There were 12d to the shilling, 20 shillings to the pound and therefore 240 old pennies to the pound. Pre-decimal currency was so easy to work with - or was it? Trams ran in Calderdale for almost 30 years. The last tram journey was on the Ovenden route on St Valentines Day (14th February), 1939.

Above: A fine old steam train pictured here pulling out of Halifax station emblazoned with the emblems of Whitakers Brewery and their Cock O'The North Ales and Stout. Was this one of the firm's specially chartered trains taking the employees and their families on their annual trip to the seaside? Or could this engine have been pulling seven large wagons filled with thousands of gallons of draught and bottled beers to Denby Dale? In September 1964, Whitakers Brewery won the contract to supply all the beer to be drunk with the giant Denby Dale Pie by an estimated crowd of 250,000 people. The dimensions of an early Denby Dale Pie, that of the 4th August, 1928, were 16 feet long, 5 feet wide and 15 inches deep.

RD Whitaker & Sons Ltd, Cock O'The North Brewery was opened in 1867 on the fringe of town, between Dean Clough and what is now, the Burdock Way roundabout. Prized for their creamy head, the XXXX bitter and Shire Ales are remembered as being stronger than many a pint today. Brewing was originally carried out in a cottage at the junction of Seedlings Mount and Crib Lane, now a much developed area, and also on the site of the old Stannary Inn which was demolished to make way for the new Halifax by-pass.

In 1959 the association of Messrs Whitbread was formed in London and two of their directors joined the Board of Whitaker's. Subsequently, in 1969, Whitaker's was sold to Whitbreads for £1,150,000. Whitakers had employed 167 people in Halifax.

Right: What an exciting place the station was at Wakes Weeks with the whole town going away on holiday. Children were warned to be careful of the carriage doors. They were dark red, solid and heavy and if they accidentally slammed on your finger...! Parents made sure the doors were securely fastened and there were blinds to pull down against the sun. Some carriages had black and white photographs of well known views and most had luggage racks of netting made with string. Some Halifax folk travelled to Fleetwood and Liverpool to catch the ferries to the Isle of Man and colourful posters on the platforms advertised seaside resorts and made claims about bracing sea air. The present Halifax station dates back to 1885 at which time the town had two other stations, North Bridge which closed in 1955 and St Pauls which closed in 1917. This photograph gives a view of the Goods Yard at Halifax Station as it used to be with the town stretching away into the distance. Upper left of this shot a corner of the Piece Hall can be seen and Square Church in its entirety stands behind the lighter coloured building. The Parish Church is shown clearly here on the right of this shot. Three of the railway lines remain but the area in the centre of this shot is now mostly car parking. Off to the right of this frame is the new Sainsbury's Store, access to the Woolshops Shopping Centre with the new Marks and Spencers store and the new Bus Station. Eureka, the museum for children under 12, is off to the left of this shot as is the bridge access to the station forecourt. Some of station platforms can be seen lower left of this picture.

Above: The size and scale of Scammonden Bridge can be seen clearly on this photograph as it spans the soon to be completed M62. The bridge, a familiar sight these days as it arches gracefully over the motorway, carries the severed ends of the old Elland to Buckstones road, (officially the A6025 Elland to Oldham road) at a height of 120 feet above the M62. Seventy miles of scaffolding had to be erected before the bridge could be built and a total of 9,000 tons of concrete were used in its construction. Scammonden is the largest, single span bridge of its type in Europe and was built at a cost of £250,000. Its vital statistics include its length of 656 feet, an arch-rib of 410 feet and a deck-length of 660 feet.

It took 18 months to build the bridge which was part of the contract for the Windy Hill to Outlane Moor stage of the M62. Standing on the bridge provides excellent views of the motorway winding west towards Lancashire and of Scammonden Dam to the east. Scammonden Dam provides water for the Huddersfield area.

The bridge was opened by Mrs Helenor Eccles, the wife of the chairman of the West Riding County Council Highways Committee, and the first wheels to cross the bridge were those of six local schoolboys on pushbikes.

Right: The mighty Scammonden bridge in the distance, Scammonden Dam can be seen middle left

of this photograph. The dam was officially opened by Her Majesty Queen Elizabeth II on October 14th 1971. The Queen observed the 1,750 million gallon dam, built by McAlpines, from a valve tower.

Now lost forever under the dam in the peaceful and pretty Deanhead Valley, the chuckling waters of the Black Brook as it flowed under the old pack-horse bridge. An old fulling mill stood near to the bridge and is now also submerged beneath the dam. The mill had not been in use for many years before the building of the dam.

Even the vast Scammonden Dam, the enlarged erstwhile Dean Head reservoir, has been known to overflow. In the 1970s torrential rain caused water to pour into the overflow at Scammonden dam, a first for many years and in sharp contrast to the drought which hit Halifax in 1996. That year saw tankers in convoy on the M62 bringing water into the town.

The sailing craft on Scammonden Water are a pleasant, (and possibly calming), sight for motorists speeding along the M62. Much enthusiasm was shown for the formation of a sailing club on Scammonden Water at a meeting held in Huddersfield Town Hall. The chairman of the steering committee made it clear that strong rules and regulations would be necessary and said, 'We must get full use out of this wonderful water, but we must be very careful and never forget that it is primarily drinking water.'

Work begins on the mighty M62, 'The Highway in the Sky', at Scammonden in 1966. The specifications for the Scammonden bridge had included instructions that it should be built to withstand windspeeds of up to 120 miles per hour and the events of Friday, November 6th, 1970 put the engineer's skill to the test. Readers may remember having read reports of the Ford Custom Cab belonging to ICB Cargo Ltd of Manchester Airport being blown onto its side against safety railings during high winds.

The driver was, fortunately, unhurt and had been returning to the airport with his unladen van. Horror awaited the Huddersfield Examiner reporter and photographer however, when they arrived at the scene to cover the story. Around a dozen tearful and terrified children, pupils of the former Dean Head School, all under 11 years of age, were attempting to fight their way across the bridge to their homes in the gale force winds.

The children travelled by mini-bus to Barkisland school after Dean Head school had been closed due to fears of a landslide following on the filling of the new Scammonden Dam but, on this occasion, the mini-bus had stopped on the other end of the bridge. The reporter, the photographer, a passing motorist, a policeman and the mother of one of the children, although barely able to stand themselves, helped the children to safety. Complaints were raised about the height of the safety railings which were subsequently raised to meet with the requests of parents and others.

The motorway was at least ten years in the planning stages before work began on this the highest motorway in the land. Mr A Kennedy, a director of Sir Alfred McAlpine & Son the contractors, is quoted as saying, 'The toughest motorway project there has been so far in Britain. The sort of challenge that civil engineers dream about....'.

Between 90,000 and 100,000 tons of Derbyshire limestone was mixed with bitumen to provide the final coating to the seven mile stretch of motorway over the moors. An estimated 11 million tons of rock were removed, principally from the moorland section and this colossal 'dig and removal' job involved the use of 40 excavators, some of them so large that they could lift ten tons in one 'scoop', 60 tractors and 70 dump-trucks. McAlpines were at one stage using 35,000 gallons of diesel each week to keep the machines moving - considerably more than was needed to keep all of Huddersfield's 'buses on the road for the same amount of time. Nine hundred men were employed at the peak of the Pennine contract and women played their part in the laboratories and offices of the project.

Sir Alfred McAlpine & Son carried out the Pennine contract and W and C French (Construction) Ltd took on the work from Outlane Moor to Leeches Hill.

The dream was realised in October, 1971 when the Queen officially opened the motorway. Now traffic can speed from Yorkshire into Lancashire where once only sheep strayed. Sheep straying onto the highway was a, potentially, highly dangerous hazard. Tests proved that even the most athletic of sheep could only manage to leap a height of 4 feet 6 inches. Fifteen miles of barrier fencing was consequently erected at a height of 4 feet 10 inches.

This aerial view of the beginnings of the M62, 'The Highway in the Sky' as it has been dubbed, shows the bridge on New Hey Road, Outlane in the foreground and Scammonden bridge in the distance, upper left hand side of the photograph. The view is westward towards Lancashire. The M62 becomes Britain's highest motorway at Windy Ridge where it reaches a maximum altitude of 1,220 feet above sea level.

This trans-Pennine motorway route runs for 50 miles and was engineered by Colonel Stuart Maynard Lovell who had the additional problematical task of designing a bridge for Scammonden which could withstand windspeeds of 120 miles per hour! A more unusual problem to face the planners was to work out how high a sheep could jump!

Scammonden Dam can be seen to the right of centre on this photograph. It is the largest rock-filled dam construction in the United Kingdom and around 6 million tons of rock 'fill' went into its creation, most of it taken from the surrounding hillsides. The Rochdale area supplied the 750,000 tons of crushed rock used to face the dam wall.

Her Majesty the Queen opened the M62 in October, 1971.

> *The M62 motorway was a feat of civil engineering with the remote pennine terrain conspiring with often difficult weather conditions. The Windy Hill section at Scammonden was probably the most challenging part to build*

Bird's eye view

This fine view shows Halifax from the south as it appeared before the outbreak of the Second World War. The picture was actually taken in the summer of 1938, almost exactly sixty years before the time of writing. The foreground of the picture is dominated by the railway station and associated goods yard. To the right of all this railway paraphernalia the Parish Church can be seen standing on a small island of land in the midst of all the industrial activity that once characterised this part of town. In the heart of the town centre, at Wards End, the newly-built A.B.C cinema looks bright in comparison to the surrounding smoke-stained buildings. Factory chimneys punctuate the skyline in almost every part of the picture a fact which emphasises the pre-smoke control era depicted by the photograph. Carpet manufacturing was well underway at Dean Clough in 1938 under the stewardship of the Crossley family. These were the days when workers at the firm proudly boasted that theirs was the largest carpet mill in the world. Readers will be able to discern many other landmarks in the photograph including Pellon Lane and Shroggs Park near the top of the scene. Halifax, along with the rest of the country was about to enter the dark wartime period which would change the lives of most of her townsfolk forever.

An aerial view of Halifax town centre in the 1950s. In the bottom right hand corner, the Piece Hall, then a fruit and vegetable market, can be quite easily seen with the spire of Square Church visible just below it. The first main road to the left of the Piece Hall is Horton Street, running downward it leads to the railway station and tracing it upward on the photograph, the junctions with Union Street and Commercial Street can be seen. At the junction with Commercial Street the large, dark, building, upper centre of the shot, is the Civic Theatre, formerly the Victoria Hall, and the open area is Wards End with Fountain Street heading upward towards Bull Green and Huddersfield Road leading off to the left. Ramsdens Brewery was at the town end of Huddersfield Road in the spot now occupied by the Halifax headquarters building. The former 'bus station, Crossfields, can be seen at the upper right hand edge of the photograph with Broad Street running in front of it. The Borough Market is in the middle of the right hand half of the shot and can be picked out by the 'dome' on its roof.

The Borough Market is a fine example of Victorian architecture much valued by the people of Halifax. It was opened in 1896 by the Duke and Duchess of York, later King George V and Queen Mary. The designers were the Leeming Bros of Halifax who planned a wide variety of fine buildings of this era including the Admiralty in London.

> *Shroggs Park was made possible by the generosity of Sir Henry Savile who leased the land to the council for 999 years at £1 a year*

The long straight road running vertically just right of centre is Ovenden Way. To the left of that is the large green rectangular area known as Ovenden Green. Rugged terraced houses form Lee Mount, and below them Ovenden Road snakes its way up towards Illingworth following the contours of the valley. This is a very rare photograph indeed, showing how the area depicted appeared before it was further developed by the Housing Department. Shroggs Park, an oasis of calm and enjoyment for many years is visible on the left. The Park was made possible through the generosity of Sir Henry Savile. He leased the land to the Corporation for 999 years for an annual rent of just £1. Many readers will remember the railway line that ran along the valley bottom and the old iron bridge (near to where the waste transfer station is today) which made a handy short cut to the late and lamented Woodside Baths. At the bottom of the picture the Canal Dyeing works and Ladyship Mills can be seen beside Old Lane, the narrow road which runs down to the Dean Clough area.

Left: This very unusual aerial view shows the centre of Halifax as it appeared in June 1964. The aircraft must have been flying on a course roughly towards the centre of town and between Hanson Lane and Pellon Lane. To the left of the bottom of Pellon Lane the bus station can be seen, with Broad Street running past it up towards Cow Green. Bull Green is the open space at the bottom of King Cross Street, a location full of character and a worthy entrance to Halifax from the route across the Pennines. Citizens from 1964 would find it hard to believe that the carefully tended round-about would eventually become home to a multi-storey car park as part of an apparent drive to make Halifax the drinking capital of the West Riding. St. Marie's church and school is visible in a location close to where Irvine Lodge started his first salon. Gibbet Street was the location for Halifax's Fire Station for many decades before the King Cross facility was built.

One striking feature of the photograph is the number of terraced houses in areas such as that adjacent to Pellon Lane. Many of these terraces have since been cleared, making way for retail parks and the new Burdock Way inner relief road.

Below: November 1961 was the date of origin for the magnificent aerial view shown here. The appearance of virtually all of the bottom left hand quarter of the photograph would be influenced by the construction of the Woolshops retail development, but not before long debates about how extensive the final plan was to be. Within this part of the picture the Lower Market can be seen, as can the abattoir and at least two large areas of derelict land which had been turned over to use as car parks. Moving towards the top of the photograph Northgate is visible and it is interesting to remember how this part of Halifax appeared before the construction of the new library and council offices. Beyond Northgate is a large open car park where later the Brunswick Bowling Alley would be built (later to be converted to the Presto, then Netto supermarket) Over the road (complete with roundabout at this time) was the Odeon cinema with adjacent Cross Field bus station. The three main streets which once unquestionably formed the retail heart of Halifax are clearly in view: Commercial Street, Market Street and Southgate. The 3D effect of this photograph almost gives the impression that one could really walk around those familiar streets and relive the atmosphere created there almost 40 years ago.

This splendid picture dates from 1962 and features dozens of interesting landmarks in the centre of Halifax. The gas and electricity works, marked by smoke and steam rising from the tall chimneys and cooling towers can be seen on the right. Below them the long viaduct carrying the railway line around the bottom of town quite close to the Parish Church and the sizeable goods yard which was adjacent to it. The tall spire of Square Church is no less impressive for not having been cleaned. Behind it the Piece Hall was in full swing as a fruit and vegetable market, long before the days when it could be considered a tourist attraction. The Town Hall looked out across an area of cleared land which was destined to become a popular indoor bowling alley (but the popularity didn't last long enough to prevent it becoming a supermarket) and the Odeon Cinema with adjacent Crossfield bus station located above them in this view. Much has been written about "The City", an area above the bus station which was characterised by closely packed housing which had a well-earned reputation for being a health hazard to anyone who lived there.

Flats were initially considered a welcome improvement on the damp and insanitary housing they replaced

This picture dates from August 1968. Mackintosh's are featured in the foreground as is the Parish Church with the electricity generating works and associated cooling towers beside it. Several blocks of flats can be seen in the picture. They were, initially at least, considered a welcome improvement on the damp and often insanitary housing they replaced by their new tenants. Just below the centre of the picture is the Piece Hall, now a popular tourist area and a busy market place on two days a week. It reopened in July 1976 as a Grade 1 listed building of architectural interest and the jewel in the crown of Halifax's tourist attractions. Obviously the Woolshops area had yet to be developed when this picture was taken and the sweeping lines of the Burdock Way were several years away from cutting a swathe through this view.

Elland from the air is featured in this picture which gives a clear view of the Gannex Mill owned by Lord Kagan, proud suppliers of distinctive raincoats to the late Labour Prime Minister the Rt, Hon. Harold Wilson. Elland is also famous for quarrying. Many Yorkshire towns have had the benefit of having their streets paved with Elland setts. Other quarried products which have found widespread use include stone roofing flags and paving stones. Huddersfield Road can be seen running from the position of the camera towards the town centre and Elland Bridge is just visible at the top right of the picture. The town centre is clearly shown and occupies the centre of the scene featured here. Elland's town Hall was opened in 1888 by Sir John Savile and the building bears his motto BE FAST. Elland's cricket field and nearby recreation ground is shown above and to the left of the town centre. They were provided for the people of the town in 1887.

The year is 1973 the photograph is an aerial shot showing the construction of the new Halifax relief road. April was an eventful month in this year as three historic events took place. On April 1st, 1973 VAT was introduced in Britain and that was no joke! Also on April 1st, the 'Big Walk' along the brand new Burdock Way attracted 20,000 participants encouraged to sample the new route on foot. And, perhaps most momentous of all, the 'Green Final' printed its final edition on April 28th. The Green Final was published by the Halifax Courier and contained sports results. Many readers may remember 'nipping down' to the shop late on a Saturday afternoon to buy a Green Final for Dad.

Burdock Way was opened on April 6th, 1973 by the Mayor of Halifax, Alderman Maurice Jagger, and the Lady Mayoress. The mayoral party included Dr Shirley Summerskill, MP for Halifax, the heads of the firms of consultant engineers and building contractors who had designed and built the roadway and Alderman John Burdock OBE after whom the road was named. The Deputy Mayor, Councillor George Smith, had the distinction of being the first person to walk on the newly-opened road.

With an hour of the road opening there was a noticeable improvement in the flow of traffic through the centre of Halifax. Burdock Way had been at least 26 years in the discussions and planning stages. Critics said that the road would 'kill' the centre of Halifax. In the event they were proved wrong. This photograph gives an aerial view of the route of the new road. The Halifax Headquarters building can be easily picked out, upper left, and beyond the Shay football ground with the speedway track around the edges of the field.

The bottom left-hand corner of this picture would be changed forever when Ramsdens Brewery was pulled down and replaced by the striking diamond shaped Halifax Building Society headquarters. Moving nearer to the town centre the Civic Theatre and A.B.C cinema stand as prominently at the end of Commercial Street as they do today. The photograph was taken in 1961, 2000 feet above the busy streets below, from a tiny single-engined aircraft slowly making its way across the skyline. Looking over towards the old bus station (now the site of the D.S.S offices) an open patch of land is visible behind the National Westminster Bank. Later a concrete office block (Crown House) and Tiffanys nightclub would occupy this position after completion in 1968. Cow Green had not yet taken on the appearance we recognise today when this picture was taken. The multi-storey car park had yet to be built and the corner of Pellon Lane and Cow Green was dominated by a large public house called the Grand Junction Hotel. It was demolished in 1968. Just in view on the right hand edge of the picture is the Piece Hall with Market Street, still completely open to traffic, above it. The Town Hall is featured in the distance, blackened by decades of sooty deposits from hundreds of mill chimneys in and around the town, but no less an imposing structure for all that.

A wealth of information is contained in this spectacular aerial view of King Cross which dates from before the construction of the Burdock Way. With so many changes it is difficult to know where to begin. Many of the houses in the top half of the picture have been cleared, including those along Skircoat Moor Road which stood on the spot which was to become the site of the new Fire Station. The construction of the Burdock Way required further house clearance, though these were generally houses which had come to the end of their useful life anyway. Right in the centre of the photograph stood the Old King public house - later demolished - with the Feathers pub and Martins Bank opposite.

This stretch of the trans-Pennine highway was a real bottleneck in the 1960s, and the problem was always exacerbated by the first falls of snow as winter approached.

On the right of the photograph Warley Road and Burnley Road appear to run parallel to each other and the old Police Station can be seen at their junction. Stanley Road veers off from Warley Road and links it to the rows of terraced housing along Fenton Road. moving further left leads to Cockroft Mann's bakery, the location of which being marked by the chimney sprouting from the centre of their premises. Moving towards the centre of the photograph from the bakery we come to a large area of land occupied by the cemetery. Even from this height one cannot fail to be impressed by the staggering number of grave stones crowded together around the tall spire of the church which once stood here.

The spire remains but the grave stones were cleared in a controversial 'landscaping' scheme a couple of decades after this picture was taken.

Below: This magnificent view dates from 1960 and shows one of the most popular residential districts of Halifax on a bright June day. Savile Park Road can be seen running from right to left just below the centre of the photograph, curving dramatically as it passes the Bell Hall area on its way to St. Judes Church and Savile Park itself. Moving upwards it is possible to see Haugh Shaw Secondary School situated on Moorfield Street.

The school closed after it became part of Halifax High School. A pity in view of the quality of the teaching staff there.

Virtually in the centre of the picture Ladyship Mills provided employment for thousands over the years and found a ready workforce in the adjacent rows of terraced houses. Of course, this was a time when motor traffic had to squeeze through King Cross and the centre of Halifax on most trans-Pennine journeys.

Many of the houses shown here would be cleared either to make way for the new relief road or as part of general improvements to the housing stock in the King Cross area.

Right: This revealing photograph gives an unusually clear impression of many well-known roads leading in and out of the town centre towards King Cross and Highroadwell. The railway station is, of course, at the bottom of the photograph with Horton Street running up in the direction of Wards End and the centre of town. Here was Ramsden's Brewery, a dark cluster of buildings which would later be cleared to allow the building of award-winning offices for the Halifax Building Society. Across the road from Ramsden's Brewery was the Labour Exchange, later to become the home of a successful insurance company.

The 'bulls eye' almost in the centre of the picture is the Bull Green roundabout, with tightly packed terraced housing shown above and to the right of it. It is easy to spot the outline of the Piece Hall, and to the right of it the abattoir on a site which would later become part of the Woolshops development. Towards the bottom left of the picture, above the railway station is New Road.

Here, in the days of the Palace Theatre, several lodging houses would be the temporary home of stars such as Frankie Vaughan. The Palace was situated at the top of Horton Street until demolition in 1959. The spot was later occupied by Halifax's Wimpy Bar and later the 'Pride of Whitby' fish restaurant.

This area has changed beyond recognition since the view was recorded almost half a century ago. The photograph was taken in 1954 high above West Vale, the photographer looking in the direction of Elland. In the foreground the neatly- walled fields clinging to the hillside would later be transformed by the construction of scores of houses. The Mount now occupies the spot nearest the camera. Most readers will be surprised to see the semi-circular outline of the mill dam on the right of the picture and the imposing mill buildings beside it.

The road linking Halifax and Stainland runs from left to right, almost horizontally through the picture. The road which begins at the bottom right of the photograph and makes its way towards the opposite corner is Saddleworth Road which follows a course taking it under the viaduct which used to carry trains on the Stainland branch line.

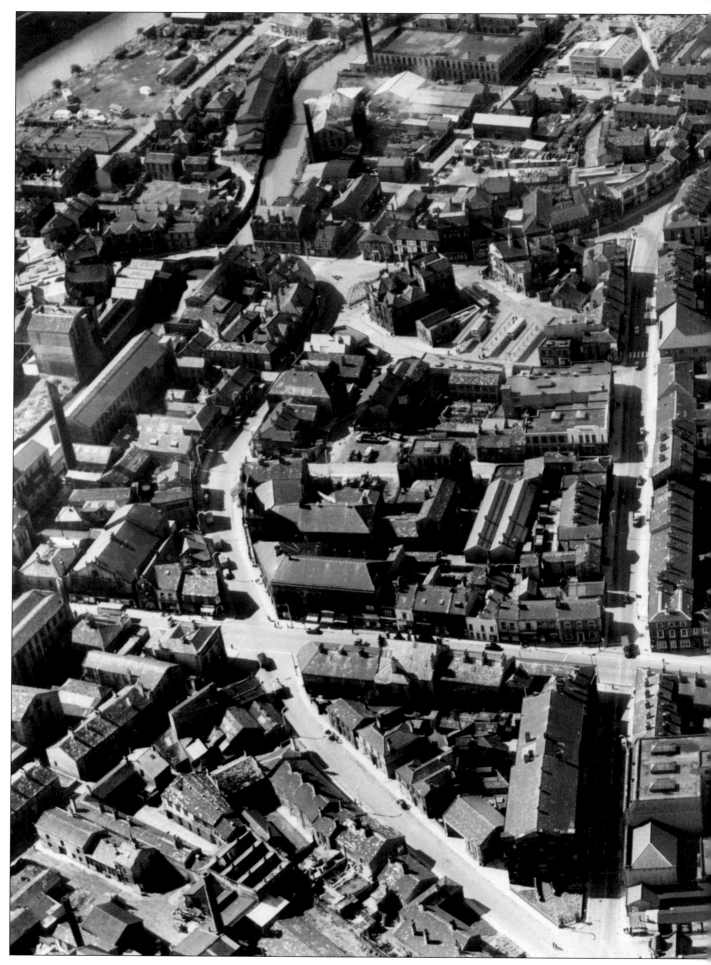

An aerial view of Brighouse in September, 1954. Bethel Street can be seen on the left of this photograph curving to the junction with Bradford Road and then on into the lower foreground of the shot. The home of the Reverend William Booth, founder of The Salvation Army, was on Bethel Street where he lived between 1857-1858. He subsequently moved to London and formed the 'Army' in 1878. In 1905 he was given a civic reception on a visit to Brighouse.

Bradford Road runs across the lower half of the frame. Sugden's Flour Mill can be seen upper left of the picture close to Bethel Street. At the left edge of this frame, a little below centre, is the area which will house the new Sainsbury's store and the buildings shown in this photograph have all been demolished.

Moving along Bradford Road from its junction with Bethel Street to the next junction, the George public house is clearly visible. In front of it, in the foreground of the picture, is the Co-op. At the top right of this photograph is the tree-covered site which became the by-pass and the 'bus station and further over, top, left of centre, is the location of Connoisseur record decks which were manufactured in the mid 1970s.

It is interesting that this should be an aerial shot of the town as Brighouse has had connections with the air and flying. In June, 1935 a group of flying enthusiasts formed the Brighouse Flying Club and 25 people attending the inaugural meeting. The Mayor of the time, Councillor A Reeve, was one of the club's keenest supporters. He was also chairman of the West Riding Joint Airport Committee.

Twenty years later, plans for a helicopter station in Brighouse were turned down by the Council Town Planning Committee. The proposed site was the junction of Mill Lane and Huddersfield Road but it was deemed to be too close to traffic on the Bradford - Huddersfield Road.

Events & occasions

This marvellous, unposed photograph is thought to date from the late 1920s or early 1930s and features a procession of civic dignitaries approaching the Parish Church. It looks like a very sombre occasion, with stern faced officials, police officers and members of the public standing in silence as the great and the good pass by. It was thought at first that this may have been the funeral of some well known local worthy, but it is more likely that the event was part of a Mayor's procession. A number of organisations are represented here including the Scouts, the Boys Brigade and smart white-gloved police officers. It is possible to pick out a group of police officers standing in a group in the distance as the last members of the party pass along the street. The street name below W.H Greenwood's own wooden sign (which, incidentally, describes them as 'top' makers) tells us that this is Alfred Street East. This can still be found on the Halifax street map of modern times, though the character of this area has seen many changes. On the right of W.H Greenwood's stood the soot-stained wool warehouse owned by Wilkinson and Wallace Ltd. Hats worn by the ladies in the picture follow the 1920s/1930s fashion of the day and fur collars are much in evidence. Medals proudly worn by the officer on the left of the photograph carry the image of Queen Victoria.

A right royal welcome

The people of Calderdale have always given a right royal welcome to their highborn visitors and the visitors seem to like it because they keep coming back for more! The visit by King George V and Queen Mary to see Dean Clough Mills, followed by lunch at Manor Heath, on July 11th, 1912, was the first of a multitude of royal visits to this area in this century.

King George VI and Queen Elizabeth's visit to Halifax in 1937.

Our reigning Monarch, Queen Elizabeth II, has visited Halifax three times. In 1949, accompanied by the Duke of Edinburgh, she came as Princess Elizabeth and inspected an exhibition of industrial products all made in Halifax. Crowds turned out to greet her and hundreds of cheering children stood on the wall of Peoples Park waving Union Jacks as she was driven by en route for the exhibition on Arden Road. As Queen she returned in 1971 and again in 1974.

This latter visit, to see the headquarters of the world's biggest building society - The Halifax - took place on a wild, windy and very wet day. The weather, however, did not dampen anyone's enthusiasm and the Queen's coral pink outfit brightened a dull day.

The Royal who is perhaps most closely linked with this area is, of course, Prince Charles. The Prince has made no less than six official visits most recently to open Eureka children's museum in 1992. Possibly the Prince's most well known visits are those which took place on St Valentines Days - 1987 and 1989. These two visits led to headlines such as, 'Valentine's Day Prince' and ' A love affair with Calderdale'. During his visit in 1987 he made a promise to return in order to visit the upper Calder Valley and he kept his promise. On February 14th,

1989, excited children waited outside Todmorden railway station with Union Jacks and welcoming home-made banners to see the Prince arrive by train. The Prince, bombarded with spring daffodils and roses which had to be carried by his bodyguards, officially opened the Woodhouse factory of Charles Openshaw & Sons Ltd. Two employees of the printing company, Mrs Tilling and Mrs Barbara Walker, presented Prince Charles with a card, chocolates, a rose and, from Mrs Walker, a peck on the cheek! He warned her that he had a cold and said he would give the chocolates to his children.

Whilst visiting Hebden Bridge Marina, the Prince boarded a narrow boat and jokingly asked if Duke, the shire horse, had ever fallen in. 'Yes, but we managed to get him out,' was the reply from Mrs Cherry Flitcroft, owner of Calder Valley Cruising.

The Royal party then moved down the valley passing through Mytholmroyd, Luddenden Foot and King Cross en route for Websters Brewery in Halifax.

Princess Anne, the Princess Royal, has visited the area almost as often as her brother and her aunt, Princess Margaret, visited the town in 1958 and 1990. The Dukes of Kent and Gloucester have both visited local industries and the Duchess of Kent, a Yorkshire lass herself, opened the Laura Mitchell Clinic on October 23rd, 1968. King Edward VIII, whilst Prince of Wales, opened Shibden Park and in October, 1937, King George VI and Queen Elizabeth, now the Queen Mother, perhaps England's favourite Royal, visited the Town Hall and drove through the town.

Below: The residents of Ovenden were among thousands of local folk who organised street parties to celebrate 'Victory in Japan Day' in August 1945. It had been a similar story in May 1945 when the country celebrated the end of the war in Europe (V.E Day). Many of the children shown here were born during the war and had known nothing but shortages and rationing during their short lives. We all know or remember anecdotes about children during the war who had never seen a banana or an orange in their lives, and it would be a long time before the shortages and rationing would come to an end. Most of the children featured in this picture will be in their 60s at the time of writing and we wonder how many of them will remember their V.J street party. Their parents had obviously pushed the boat out for the occasion and many of them were content to look on while the youngsters enjoyed the late summer treat. Children today might be expected to giggle at the v-signs being made by their predecessors. The gesture would be rather less welcome today at respectable gatherings in the town. The cheeky two fingered salute was made famous by Winston Churchill, but is thought to originate from the battle of Agincourt when the bow fingers of captured archers were cut off in order to render them useless in battle. Archers who escaped the cruel practice are said to have waved their healthy bow fingers defiantly at the enemy and the familiar salute sprang up from there.

Right: The war effort in 1939-1940 and the citizens of Halifax, as they are being encouraged to give, are being reminded of the price other citizens have paid by the slogan at the back of the dais. This appears to be an auction and the blackboard, in front of the auctioneer, the Mayor of Halifax Alderman George Barker, tells us that 'plants, china etc' will be auctioned at 10.30 followed by Freehold Property and Livestock at 2.30 and 3.0 respectively. Hats and hairstyles in the audience are very much of the period and the faces in the room are reflected in the mirror for sale, upper left of the picture.

Halifax people gave to the war effort in a multitude of ways. The young women of the town were 'called up' to join the Land Army, the Armed Forces or work in engineering or munitions factories. Several Halifax girls went to work at ROF, (Royal Ordinance Factory), Chorley and were involved in highly dangerous work with explosives. The whole of the factory was underground and the girls had to wear special clothing, asbestos suits which made their skin itch. They had to wear specially made hand-sewn shoes and jewellery was absolutely forbidden apart from wedding rings which could be carried in a bag around their necks. Disturbing and distressing was the number written on the knee of each employees asbestos suit - for identification in case of explosive accident. The girls who worked in TNT and cordite sections suffered their skins turning bright yellow and their hair turning green.

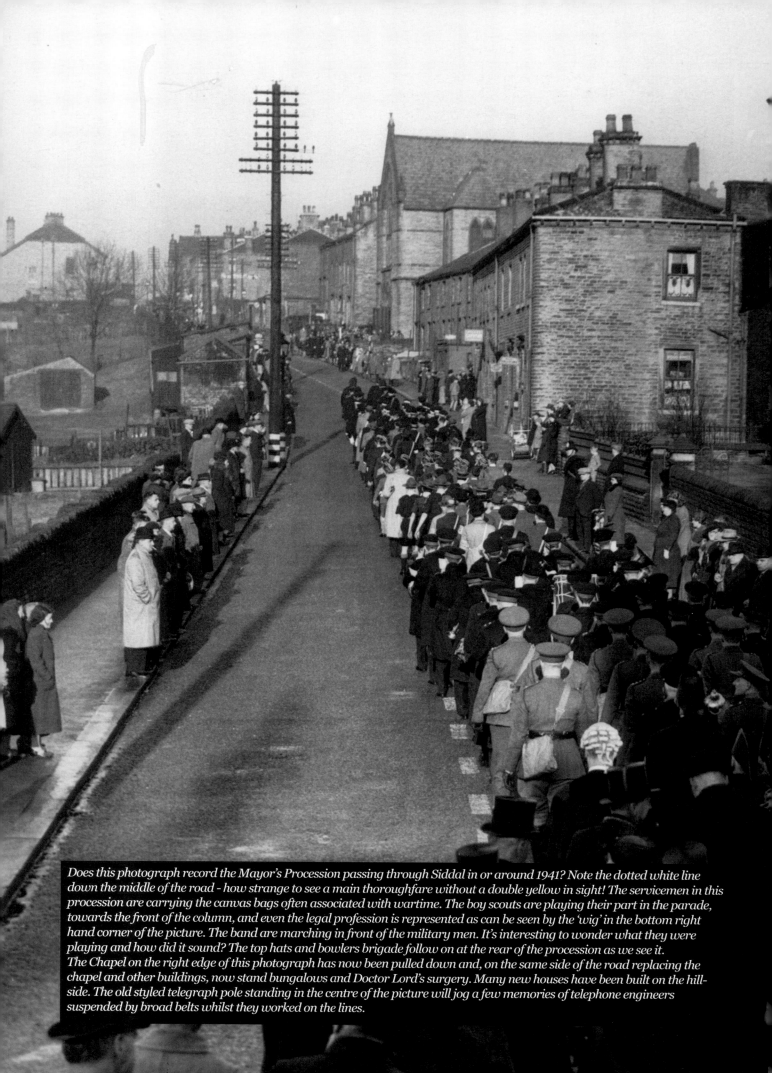

Does this photograph record the Mayor's Procession passing through Siddal in or around 1941? Note the dotted white line down the middle of the road - how strange to see a main thoroughfare without a double yellow in sight! The servicemen in this procession are carrying the canvas bags often associated with wartime. The boy scouts are playing their part in the parade, towards the front of the column, and even the legal profession is represented as can be seen by the 'wig' in the bottom right hand corner of the picture. The band are marching in front of the military men. It's interesting to wonder what they were playing and how did it sound? The top hats and bowlers brigade follow on at the rear of the procession as we see it.

The Chapel on the right edge of this photograph has now been pulled down and, on the same side of the road replacing the chapel and other buildings, now stand bungalows and Doctor Lord's surgery. Many new houses have been built on the hillside. The old styled telegraph pole standing in the centre of the picture will jog a few memories of telephone engineers suspended by broad belts whilst they worked on the lines.

Above: An example of one way in which the people of Halifax did their bit for the war effort. Illustrated here are items donated for sale to raise money and the people who helped by both giving and buying. The child's potty chair in the bottom left hand corner of the photograph may appear strange to the young Mums of today and how many homes still boast a piano? The words of the old song, 'She was only a bird in a gilded cage', come to mind when looking at the two bird cages on display here and it appears, centre back of the picture, that the Devil himself may have helped to celebrate the takings! Ivory tusks feature to the right of the shot and a well worn cane-bottomed chair is up for auction in the bottom right hand corner. In 1940 a gentleman helper called into the Comforts Fund Centre in Halifax to donate four knitted helmets and two knitted pairs of gloves. This brought his contribution over a period of one month to 20 pairs of gloves and four helmets! The Halifax Comforts Fund had appealed for people to knit items and handed out patterns as required. The knitted items together with other 'comforts' were parcelled up and sent to Halifax soldiers overseas.

Knitting was a popular and practical pastime and there were many wool shops in the town centre. Can readers remember knitting fine garments for babies in two-ply wool? Knitting socks for husbands and sons, (or wives and daughters), and 'turning' the heel? There was also a time when people darned socks!

Below left: A group of very well dressed youngsters here, gloves and handbags, the boys in suitably masculine and gentlemanly poses, a handkerchief in the top pocket of the young man to the back right of the photograph. Not a single pair of grey knee socks, as worn by the lads, has been allowed to slide and fall wrinkled around the ankles. Well behaved boys indeed!

The date of this picture is judged to be late 1940s - early 1950s but the occasion remains a mystery. The shield would indicate that the young people pictured have won some kind of annual award. If this were a school group there would surely be a teacher present? If a church group surely a vicar, priest or Sunday School teacher would be there? It seems unlikely that this shot represents an outing or visit.

These young women would come to know that 'Friday night is Amami night'! They may have later worn 'glass' stockings with seams and tried to figure out 'which twin has the Toni?'! Proud Mums could have washed the gleaming white socks worn by the girls in Oxydol and darned holes in those worn by the boys using a darning 'mushroom' and grey darning wool.

Below: When King George VI and his Queen Elizabeth, now the Queen Mother, visited Halifax in October, 1937, the Queen wore a two piece dress in a beige-pink pastel shade with a three-quarter length coat trimmed with fox fur. She wore a modern hat with a high crown which was trimmed with light fawn velvet. The royal couple were spending a few days visiting Yorkshire and, on the day they came to Halifax, October 20th, a 21-gun salute roared out a welcome from Beacon Hill and smiling, waving crowds thronged the route.

The King and Queen stayed with the Princess Royal and Lord Harewood at Harewood House for the duration of their visit to Yorkshire and the Princess Royal accompanied them to Halifax. The Princess was a regular visitor to our town, this was her sixth trip, and massed schoolchildren cheered and waved at the royal party when they drove along Savile Park. Halifax has always been popular with royal visitors.

King George V and Queen Mary, as Duke and Duchess of York, came to open the Borough Market and the Royal Halifax Infirmary in 1896. It had been intended that the Infirmary would be known as the 'Halifax Royal Infirmary' but the Duke of York slipped up in his speech and inadvertently named it the 'Royal Halifax Infirmary' and that it has remained ever since.

Right: Definitely the 'Havercake Lads' in this photograph, the elephant badges on their lapels and their cap badges identify them clearly as members of the Duke of Wellington's Regiment. The gentleman in 'civvies' picking up a cup of tea, looks like Alderman George Barker JP who became Mayor of Halifax in November 1939. The photograph is likely to date from 1939-40 and the location is possibly the Exchange Restaurant which used to be near the Town Hall.

Have the lads invited the Mayor to a company 'smoker'? How many readers have attended those events and how many readers can still the remember the morning after? Or is this a more formal affair, were the lads being treated to a slap up civic meal before returning to the fighting?

The Dukes have been dubbed the 'Havercake Lads' as a result of recruiting sergeants traditionally carrying a 'havercake' on the end of their bayonets. A havercake is basically oatbread.

The 'Havercake Lads' have a long and lasting relationship with Halifax. On March 9th, 1944 they were featured in a series of wartime radio broadcasts which paid tribute to famous British regiments. The programme highlighted the more famous incidents from the history of the 'Havercake Lads' and referred to distinguished action at Dunkirk. The 1st Battalion held a two mile front for five days allowing the evacuation to take place and was the last unit to leave.

Above: This bonny little boy surrounded by caring nurses and cuddly toys is on Rawson Ward at the Royal Halifax Infirmary during or just after the second World War. This ward was described as 'Open Air' because all the windows could be opened onto the veranda and some of the children, dependant on their ailment, slept on the veranda. What appears to be a drip stand beside the little boy's bed could have been there to give him fluids. In those day fluids would have been admitted through the scalp or the rectum as the necessary technology for venous access was not available. Fluids would be administered in cases of dehydration which could have been caused by vomiting, the inability to drink or high temperatures. There were no antibiotics in those days and Penicillin was only just becoming widely available.

There are an awful lot of toys for one small boy's bed in this photograph which could mean that the picture commemorates a donation of toys to the Infirmary. The Royal Halifax Infirmary was built on voluntary donations and the plaques outside each ward name the benefactor who paid, an average, £5,000 endowment. When the new Halifax hospital opens in 2001/2 it is hoped that the Infirmary plaques will be transferred and used. Former staff of the Royal Halifax Infirmary are hoping that an archive room may be made available to display interesting artefacts, silver and both still and moving film of the RHIs fascinating history. The RHI was opened in 1896 by the Duke and Duchess of York. It is the Royal Halifax rather than the Halifax Royal because the Duke made a mistake when declaring the building open!

Above: Children of the 1940s in their best bibs and tuckers but pinpointing this photograph exactly is difficult. The children appear to be fit and healthy which would indicate that they are on an escorted tour or outing. An official air is added to the scene by the presence of the Mayor in the background. On the right of the picture, the scarf-like white headgear of the senior nurse would indicate an Assistant Matron at the Halifax General Hospital. The building in the background, the gravel in the foreground and the presence of nurses adds strength to the opinion that this photograph was taken at what used to be the front entrance to the Halifax General Hospital.

The hospital opened in 1801 and was originally a workhouse. There has always been a great deal of rivalry between the nurses who trained at the Royal Halifax Infirmary and nurses who trained at the 'General' which probably has its roots in days of the workhouse.

Children's wards in the 1940s and 50s were in complete contrast to the children's wards of today. The children were required to stay in their beds, toys were few and far between and the walls were plainly painted. Today's children meet a riot of colour in their hospital ward. They can be noisy and run around and there are lots of toys and activities.

A nurses least favourite job in the 1950s to 60s would be cleaning! The Royal Halifax Infirmary, in these days before central heating, had a chimney in the centre of each ward with a fireplace at each side. The nurses had to first sweep the ward and then stoke the fire.

Below: The children's ward at the Royal Halifax Infirmary during or immediately after World War II. The nurses uniforms date the photograph as pre-1950, and this is, therefore, likely to be Rawson Ward. Nurses continued to wear starched collars into the 1950s but they were narrower than the ones shown here and cuffs were not worn on the arms. The starched aprons in this shot are worn around the neck whereas later ones are pinned to the bodice. Student nurses in the 1950s wore pale blue and white striped dresses with starched white collars, aprons and hats and each of these latter items was ironed separately by hospital laundry staff. Nurses in their third year of training reached the dizzy heights of purple and white striped dresses, wearing them gave the nurses a sense of pride and self-importance. On qualification and becoming Staff Nurses, a purple belt was added to the dress and a smaller, more elaborate hat was worn. The hat was a square of fabric with cotton pulled to create pleats at the back and there had to be 15 pleats. Nursing sisters wore, (and still wear), dark blue whilst Matron wore a plain dark green dress with a white hat made of lightly patterned muslin. This photograph with its two bonny babies could have been taken in the corridor or just inside the ward entrance. Sister Tutor can be seen second from right in her distinctive 'bonnet' hat and the plaque on the wall is likely to have been brought from the original Infirmary building in Dispensary Walk.

Did Teletubbies originate in the Royal Halifax Infirmary? If not what is that toy in the centre of the picture?

The Duke of Wellington's Regiment

The feeling of belonging which has always existed between the 'Dukes' and the people of Halifax probably dates back to the 1760s. Lord Cornwallis, commanding troops in the American War of Independence, decided upon the West Riding as the area from which he would recruit men into his regiment, the 33rd Regiment of foot. From that moment on, the regiment became tied to this area and known as the 33rd or 1st Yorkshire West Riding Regiment. To this day, there are few local families who do not have a relative who is, or was, a member of the regiment.

A young man named Arthur Wellesley joined the Regiment as a major in 1793 and took over as colonel of the 33rd or 1st Yorkshire West Riding Regiment in 1806. In 1813 he was asked by the monarch to command the horseguards and the monarch could not be refused! The regiment and their colonel had to part company.

Arthur Wellesley (1st Duke of Wellington) met up with the regiment again at the Battle of Waterloo and due to the close relationship which had existed between them, the 33rd asked to be named The Duke of Wellington's Regiment. The Dukes are the only regiment in the British Army to be named after a person who is not of royal blood.

The celebrations for the 250th anniversary of the Duke of Wellington's Regiment, 1702 - 1952.

The Dukes have been involved in fighting Britain's battles from the War of Spanish succession, (1702-1713), to the more recent conflict in the Balkans where they played an important role. They have served in the American War of Independence, (1775-1783), the Napoleonic Wars, (1793-1815), the Crimea, (1854-1856), the Boer War, (1899-1902), the Great War, (1914-1918), World War II, (1939-1945) and all the intervening conflicts.

During the recent hostilities in the Balkans, one Corporal Mills of the Duke of Wellington's Regiment was the first soldier to be awarded the new Conspicuous Gallantry Cross. This latter is a new medal introduced by the Queen in 1993 for bravery on the battlefield. There is only one higher award for bravery - the Victoria Cross.

On the 18th of June, 1815 was fought the battle which was ever to be associated with the Duke of Wellingtons - the Battle of Waterloo. The battle lasted all day and Napoleon is reported to have said, 'These dogs of English never know when they are beaten.' That could have been, of course, because they weren't beaten and the rest, as they say, is history.

Above: The boys in blue here marching smartly through the streets followed by flag bearing boy scouts. This photograph is believed to date back to 1935 and the Silver Jubilee celebrations. Or could it be an early picture of Compo, Foggy and Clegg on a visit to the town? Note the flat-capped observers on the far right of the shot. May 6th, 1935 was the 25th anniversary of the accession to the throne of King George V following the death of his father, King Edward VII and, what is now, Calderdale celebrated in style with processions, bonfires, tumblers and acrobats, tree planting and community singing. In the modern day jargon of television, there is a 'link' here. The Halifax Police Station used to be on Harrison Road in the building which was once the Infirmary. The Infirmary's new building on Free School Lane was opened in 1896 by King George V and Queen Mary when they were Duke and Duchess of York! Within a week of the new 30 mph speed limit being introduced, March 18th 1935, a local policeman on patrol at Cote Hill arrested the first person in the Borough to be caught offending! The speedster, from Bradshaw, had been seen driving his motorbike towards King Cross at speeds of up to 40mph. The accused pleaded 'not guilty m'lud' but was nevertheless found guilty and fined £1. The bike rider did not have a speedometer and said to buy one would cost more than his bike was worth. The new Halifax Police Station is located at Richmond Road, off Pellon Lane.

Top: Crowds line the route as Halifax's own regiment, the Duke of Wellington's, march through the streets on Waterloo Day, June 18th, 1945. The parade is seen here marching from the direction of Wards End towards Bull Green where they are to be honoured with the Freedom of the County Borough of Halifax. Looking down towards Wards End, the Victoria Hall, now the Civic Theatre, can be seen against the skyline, centre left of the photograph. At the turn of the century it was decided that the development of the town centre needed a centrepiece, a visible symbol of the new civic pride.

The Victoria Hall was designed to be that centrepiece and was erected in a prime spot at the junction of Commercial Street and Fountain Street. The magnificent building in late English Renaissance style was built in 1900 and officially opened in February, 1901. The large floor was a talking point in those days. It is supported entirely on special springs and was a totally new feature all those years ago.

Dr Hans Richter conducted a combined orchestra for the gala occasion and the excellent acoustics were demonstrated by a performance given by the Halifax Choral Society. Some 90 years later the floor held up under jiving in the aisles to the Bootleg Beatles and the acoustics have done justice on many occasions over the years to the pantomime shouting of 'Oh yes he is. Oh no he isn't!'

Above: Halifax honours its Regiment and a crowded Bull Green is the venue. Waterloo Day, 1945 is the date, (June 18th), and Colonel CJ Pickering can be seen, inset, receiving the Deed of Grant of the Freedom of the Borough from the Mayor, Alderman L Chambers JP.

Bollards and the old black and white 'Keep Left' signs and, later, a large and flowery roundabout have occupied the space used by the crowd in upper right quarter of this photograph. Further changes in 1998 will alter Bull Green once again. The Lewins public house, whose once upon a time 'men only' policy was breached by a young Halifax woman dressed as a man, was situated to the left of this shot. The Lewins is now O'Neills. Public lavatories which once stood Ladies on one side, Gents on the other of the steps in front of Bull Green House were converted into the appropriately named WCs Bar! The name has since been changed but the bar remains in business.

Businesses of the time which can be seen on this photograph include Sutcliffes Hairdressers, J Woodhead & Co and W Workman & Co.

Above right: An amazing scene at Bull Green on June 18th 1945. A crowd of thousands had turned out to see the Mayor of Halifax hand over the Freedom of the Borough to the Duke of Wellington's Regiment. People sat precariously on every ledge and can be seen right of centre of this photograph perched above a shop. Freedom of the Borough gave the Dukes the right to march through the town with bayonets fixed, Colours flying and bands playing on all ceremonial occasions. The circle inset in the right hand corner of this photograph is The Duke of Wellington. The inset on the left shows No. 5891907 Private Richard Burton VC. Private Burton was awarded his VC as a result of action in Italy on October 8th 1944. The Dukes had moved forward to capture a vital 'feature' which stood 760 metres high. The 'feature' had to be taken as it dominated the immediate vicinity and Private Burton dashed forward alone and on his own initiative four times. When the ammunition in his Tommy-gun ran out, he picked up a Bren gun and fired with great accuracy from the hip. To quote the London Gazette of January, 1945, 'Private Burton's magnificent gallantry and total disregard of his own safety during many hours of fierce fighting in mud and continuous rain were an inspiration to all his comrades.'

Ten 'Dukes' have received Victoria Cross citations and three are displayed in the Regimental museum at Bankfield Museum. Corporal Mills of the Duke of Wellington's Regiment was awarded the Conspicuous Gallantry Cross for bravery on the battlefield during the recent hostilities in the Balkans.

A festive Southgate in celebration of the end of the war in Europe is shown here - VE Day, May 8th, 1945. What a maelstrom of emotions this day must have brought to the people of the town. Elation at the ending of six long years of war, of saying goodbyes to loved ones, of listening to wartime announcements on the radio. Sadness with the thoughts of those who would never come back, those who hadn't survived to see this day - the soldiers, the airmen, the sailors, the munitions workers, the civilians killed by bombs. Feelings of intense relief that at last life could begin to return to normal.

Six weeks after this photograph was taken, the Prime Minister, Winston Churchill visited Halifax and was met by a crowd of beaming faces. With his familiar cigar clamped between his teeth, he toured the town in an open-topped car flanked by two security men in civilian clothes.

On the right hand side of this photograph the old Boars Head Hotel can be seen. Many readers will remember Berni Inns, the downstairs bar and steak and chips in the 1960s. Marks and Spencers, before their extension was built, can be seen opposite the hotel. Marks and Spencers opened their store here in 1933. The Rose and Crown, a Whitakers public house, was adjacent to Marks and Spencers but was demolished to make way for the expansion of the famous store.

Above: It is the 18th of June, 1945, the 130th anniversary of the Battle of Waterloo, the place is Bull Green and the occasion is the granting of the Freedom of the County Borough of Halifax to the Duke of Wellington's Regiment. The Colonel of the Regiment, General Pickering, can be seen on the dais together the Mayor of Halifax. Freedom of the Borough means that the Regiment, officers and other ranks, can, on all ceremonial occasions, pass through the town with bayonets fixed, Colours flying and bands playing. This they did seven years later in celebration of their 250th anniversary. The Duke of Wellington's Regiment has survived the severe cuts in the strength of the Army which have resulted in the disbandment or amalgamation of many famous regiments since the end of the Second World War. The Dukes will now remain in the order of battle of the British Army for the foreseeable future. A small Regimental Headquarters still occupies a part of the barracks at Highroad Well and the Dukes continue to recruit most of their soldiers from this area. The Regimental Museum is held as part of Bankfield Museum, Boothtown and the Regimental Chapel and memorials are in the Chapel of Resurrection in Halifax Parish Church. Since World War II the Dukes have served with the United Nations Forces in Cyprus and Korea. Here, the 1st Battalion gained Battle Honour 'The Hook 1953' for their determined defence against an overwhelming Chinese attack. The Dukes also served throughout the Commonwealth, in Germany and in Northern Ireland.

Right: What could be more fitting than to grant the Freedom of the County Borough of Halifax to the Duke of Wellingtons Regiment on the 130th anniversary of the Battle of Waterloo. The battle with which they will forever be associated and after which they officially became the 'Dukes'.

These soldiers, their faces showing the solemnity of the honour to be conferred upon them, were standing before the saluting dais in Bull Green. Their cap badges, made of bakelite in this shot due to wartime shortages, replicate the crest of the Duke of Wellington. The motto 'Virtutis Fortuna Comes', (Fortune Favours the Brave), appears on the cap badges and beneath the crest is a scroll bearing the words 'West Riding'. The badge of an elephant inscribed with the word 'Hindoostan' is worn on the collar and is also seen on the regimental buttons.

Halifax Parish Church contains the Regimental Chapel in the Chapel of Resurrection. The only memorial in the chapel is a roll of honour listing the names of those who were killed in the Second World War and the 37 soldiers who died in Korea. Elsewhere in the Church are other memorials remembering those who died in the Boer War and the First World War.

The Battle of Waterloo took place on June 18th 1815. Reports of the battle refer to 'British squares', meaning traditional defence formations. But, in modern day parlance, would anyone describe fighting soldiers as 'British squares'?

Below: Spit and polish was no doubt the order of the day for these men of the Duke of Wellingtons Regiment on this occasion. Rifles will have been cleaned, buttons and brass made to gleam, berets adjusted to just the right angle and belts 'blanco'd' to perfection.

Field-marshal Viscount Montgomery of Alamein, Chief of the Imperial General Staff is seen in this photograph on a routine visit to 33 PTC, (Primary Training Centre), at Wellesley Barracks on November 3rd, 1947. This same visit to Halifax included an inspection of the Royal Army Service Corps, Ovenden Camp. At the time this photograph was taken Field-marshal Montgomery held the rank of general.

The soldier shaking hands with the General is well decorated as can be seen from the medal ribbons on his chest. Could this be the subject of their conversation?

The Halifax Courier and Guardian of the time reported a little known link between the Field-marshal and Halifax. To quote the newspaper, 'His mother was the daughter of Dean Farrar, famous author of 'Life of Christ' and 'Eric', who in turn was the grandson of Jonathan Farrar the Luddenden and Warley clock and watch maker.'

In the background of this shot, upper right hand corner, can be seen the building which was once the Officers Mess. Wellesley Barracks remains the regimental headquarters of the Duke of Wellingtons Regiment although nowadays they only occupy one building. The remainder of Wellesley Park is used by the peripatetic teaching services of the local authority. Nevertheless, to the people of Halifax, the castellated stone building at Highroad Well is, and always will be, simply 'The Barracks'.

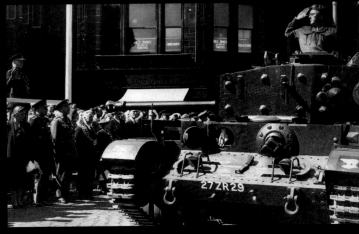

Above: A gloriously sunny Saturday in May 1952 and the whole town turns out to celebrate with the Duke of Wellington's Regiment. The cause for the two-day party? The 250th anniversary of the Regiment, 1702 - 1952. Avid onlookers can be seen on the roof of CW Gledhill's and leaning out of windows on the second floor of the building in the upper left hand corner of the photograph. The parade has moved past the top of Crown Street and is moving along Commercial Street near to the bottom of George Square. Lt-Colonel FJ Crossley, MBE, TD, can be seen here leading the 382nd Field Regiment, RA, Duke of Wellington's in the parade which ended with a display in Manor Heath. An estimated crowd of 5,000 watched the display in the park. To the left of the photograph, each side of Lt-Colonel Crossley, can be seen signs for 'Tetley Cigarettes' and Smith's Dyers. A dry-cleaning business has remained in those premises to this day. Immediately to the right of the tank, central to the photograph, can be seen the striped awning of Asquith's shop, well known in the town for their chic and stylish handbags and umbrellas. A little further along, the first white awning shades the products in the window of L. Ainley, Cigars and Tobacco and the jutting sign for 'State Express 555'. No restrictions on tobacco advertising in the 1950s! The old style 'No Waiting' sign, left of centre in the photograph, applies to traffic and not, of course, the crowd!

Above right: The Duke of Wellington takes the salute from Lt-Colonel FJ Crossley in his comet tank during the celebratory parade of May 24th, 1952 - the 250th anniversary of the Duke of

Wellington's regiment. As can be seen from the street sign, top centre of the photograph, the saluting dais was positioned at the bottom of George Square. Subsequent Dukes of Wellington, after the 1st Duke, Arthur Wellesley, have held the rank of Colonel in Chief of the Regiment but only if the appointment has been appropriate. The present Duke is Colonel in Chief and was previously a brigadier in the army. The Mayor of Halifax, (Alderman W Regan, himself an old 'Duke'), can be seen at the saluting dais and the mayors and mayoresses of Huddersfield, Brighouse and Mossley were also amongst the dignitaries on that day. General Sir Philip Christison, the much respected and well liked Colonel of the Regiment, the Earl of Scarborough, Lord Lieutenant of Yorkshire (West Riding) and Lord Savile were also present. The names of Rice, Jones & Smith, Solicitors, are still written in gold on the first floor windows of Albany Chambers. Below their offices was Collingwoods the Jewellers now this spot is occupied by the Halifax Estate Agency. The 'Dukes' will be celebrating their 300th anniversary in the year 2002.

A sunny and ceremonial Saturday afternoon in Halifax in May, 1952. This year saw Princess Elizabeth become Queen Elizabeth II, Sovereign of the United Kingdom and of the British Commonwealth and Empire, succeeding her father King George VI. A year later was the coronation and also the conquering of Everest for the first time by Sir Edmund Hillary and Sherpa Tensing who were members of Colonel John Hunt's expedition. Seven earlier attempts had failed, some with loss of life. This photograph taken, at the bottom of George Square looking down Commercial Street, shows the Territorial Army Band under the leadership of Bandmaster F Ashton-Jones. The huge crowds which turned out for the event can be seen on the photograph with one man climbing onto the roof of Gledhill Hosier, right hand side of the picture. The stack of the old Odeon cinema can be seen in the distance, centre right, and the Yorkshire Penny Bank building is in front. The parade of shops on the right of the shot included Asquith's umbrella and handbag shop, and Ainley's tobacconist who sported a sign advertising State Express 555 cigarettes. Cheapside meets Commercial Street at around this point and readers may remember Lileys pram and toy shop which occupied the corner plot for many years. The site is now used by Klick Photopoint and Specsavers. Marks and Spencers were associated with Cheapside until their move in 1998.

A grand spectacle for the people of Halifax on this occasion - the celebrations of the 250th anniversary of Halifax's own Duke of Wellington's Regiment. For the first time since Waterloo Day, (June 18th), 1945 the Dukes exercised their right to march through the town with bayonets fixed, Colours flying and bands playing. The date is the 24th May, 1952. This photograph shows Lt-Colonel JF Crossley, MBE, TD, in his comet tank leading the 382nd Field Regiment, RA, Duke of Wellington's. The 24th May that year dawned hot and sunny and the people of the town turned out in their thousands to celebrate with the Dukes. The parade began at 2 pm, the crowds, an hour earlier, were already estimated at 20,000. This shot was taken at the top of Crown Street which can be seen leading downward from the left hand side of the photograph. Can any readers spot themselves in the crowd? The highway is paved with 'sets' and the zebra crossing in the bottom right hand corner would have had a belisha beacon at each end.

The Dukes regimental museum is housed at Bankfield Museum in Akroyd Park and has exhibits covering all the major exploits of the 'Havercake Lads.' The regiment will celebrate its 300th anniversary in 2002 and, although the style of the celebration has not yet been decided, the people of the town will no doubt play a part.

Above: The well turned out and well drilled men of Regimental HQ and Depot, The Duke of Wellington's Regiment, Training Company, photographed on May 24th 1952 when the Dukes celebrated their 250th anniversary. They are seen marching along Huddersfield Road.

The youthful faces which can be seen in this parade indicate that they are recent recruits who have probably just completed basic training. What happened to them? Between 1945 and 1987 the Dukes went soldiering all around the world. 1953 saw the notorious Battle of the Hook in Korea and the Dukes duties also included the defence of the West, duties in the Commonwealth, internal security duties in Northern Ireland and support for the United Nations. Regimental Headquarters remain here in Halifax at Wellesley Barracks, the last vestige of the old barracks which was once fully occupied by the Duke's men.

Currently, the 1st Battalion move around on an 'arms plot' and are at present based in Hounslow undertaking public duties in London, for example guarding Buckingham Palace. The Territorial Army Battalion, called the 3rd Battalion, have companies based in the Drill Hall in Halifax with detachments in Keighley, Huddersfield, Barnsley and Sheffield.

Right: No-one had heard of 'aerobics' or 'step' in the 1960s when this photograph was taken. Going to the gym only really happened at school whilst wearing baggy grey gym knickers and an aertex shirt or perhaps woolly pleated 'shorts' which came down to the knees and looked like a skirt. No-one popped down to the gym after work and few people owned brightly coloured lycra leotards. Fish and chips were fried in fat and 'polyunsaturates' meant nothing!

These pupils from Rishworth School together with a visiting Swiss team, were giving a gymnastic display in Southgate watched by a crowd which included the Mayor and Mayoress. This photograph shows the finale. Note the fashionable flares worn by the young lady fifth from the right at the upper right hand corner of this shot.

Southgate at this time was open to two-way traffic, it became 'pedestrianised' in 1973. Moores Tobacconist was at one time on the corner of Southgate and Westgate. Fred Moores electrical appliances shop is one of those to have moved out of the precinct area. Irvine Hindle the jewellers have gone and Moodies, also jewellers, have moved into their old premises.

Ryley & Sons the stationers established in 1895 stood on the precinct alongside Hindles until 1991. Readers will remember buying a special pencil, pen or notebook in

Ryleys, climbing the old linoleum covered stairs with the well worn wooden handrail to the well stocked upper floor and browsing through the goods on display. There was something special about starting a new page in a new exercise book!

Above: The Lady Mayoress of Halifax, (the wife of Alderman Maurice Jagger), is seen here at a Red Cross Food Fair in 1973. The home-made cakes are mouth-watering and presumably baked by some of the ladies seen in this shot. It is surprising how many of the donated products displayed in the foreground are still around today. HP sauce, Campbell soup, brandy snaps and 'All Butter Sultana Cookies' from Marks and Spencers - although they were only 9p for 12 in those days! At the edge of the table there stands a packet of Bisto, remember the Bisto Kids? Ah..Bisto!

The International Red Cross was formed in 1864 by a Swiss man named Henry Dunant. By signing up to the Geneva Convention, countries agree to protect wounded soldiers and the people who care for them. All buildings, ships, aircraft, ambulances and trains marked with the red cross are to be considered free from attack, providing they do not contain troops or war supplies. The Red Cross also helps families separated by war to trace relatives, cares for refugees and comes to the assistance of those who are hurt or homeless because of floods, earthquakes or other disasters.

Below: It's Punch Bowl Motors on the road out of Boothtown, leading towards Queensbury and eventually Bradford, and it's Alderman and Mrs Maurice Jagger, Mayor and Lady Mayoress of Halifax, receiving a Dutch Gouda cheese from an attractive young woman in traditional Dutch costume. The smiling young lady could have been of Dutch nationality because the event pictured is connected with the promotion of DAF cars which were originally manufactured in Holland. DAF were subsequently bought out by Volvo, the Swedish company. Could the smiles in the photograph be in any way connected with comments about 'cheesy' grins?

Shopping spree

Mr Owen Sellers, the son of the famous and talented photographer JT Sellers, still lives in Luddenden Foot and has fond memories of his father. He remembers him as a quiet man with a dry sense of humour. As well as his talent, some would say genius, for photography, Mr JT Sellers was skilled in may other ways. He could mend watches and was something of a musician. Whenever he set foot in a local pub he would always be asked to 'give 'em a tune' on the piano or organ. Owen remembers that when a girl from the Salvation Army went into a pub he would strike up 'The Old Rugged Cross' and insist that the girl sang it before any donations could be collected! Owen still has a map which belonged to his father and on which his father had ringed every town and village he had visited in the course of his photographic work. This covered the whole of Great Britain. In those days glass negatives were used which were, of course, extremely heavy. Put their weight and bulk together with the size and weight of the camera and tripod and you have quite a load to carry to, for example, a remote part of Scotland. Lilywhite's therefore used to post the glass negatives 'poste restante' for Mr Sellers to collect on arrival. Sometimes he had to hire a cycle or climb a mountain to get the shot he wanted, lenses then were not what they are today.

Below: There have been many changes in the King Cross area over the years, but by and large the main shopping street has retained the general character and appearance depicted here. King Cross is still a busy shopping area, though some traders voice concern about new shopping facilities which seem to threaten their livelihoods. At the time this picture was taken, in the 1950s, these thoughts would have been far from the minds of the shopkeepers who ran these well-patronised shops. These were the days before the large 'weekly shop' carried out with the help of the family saloon and the local supermarket. 'Shopping' was more spread out throughout the week and took on something of a social ritual where personal preferences were remembered by attentive shop keepers and everyone seemed to have time for a smile and a kind word. Thankfully one can still find these standards of service in King Cross as in the rest of the district - if you look for it. King Cross was usually very busy with 'through' traffic, travelling up and down the Calder Valley and along Rochdale Road to Sowerby Bridge and over the Pennines to Lancashire. The photographer had obviously chosen a quieter moment to capture this view for us to enjoy today.

Above: If the clock in this photograph is showing the correct time, (11.40 am) we have a gloomy morning on Horton Street in the 1940s here. A fine collection of Austin cars grace the first floor of Greenwoods showroom and a Rover is parked on the roadside, right hand edge of the picture. A quality furniture shop, a home decoration shop and a branch of Argos now stand on the sites once occupied by Greenwoods and WL Pawson Gown Manufacturers.

The function of the attractively, ornate post, right of centre in this shot, is a mystery. If it were connected with trams there would surely be a cable linking this post to the next one? If it were some kind of street light why is it sited within yards of a gas lamp?

The gas street lamp, left of centre in this photograph, will strike a chord in many readers' memories. They used to cast a special glow, a yellowish, soft pool of light which many describe as sinister and evocative of films about Victorian murderers such as Jack the Ripper. Young women of Halifax were frightened with stories of 'The Halifax Slasher' in the period immediately before the Second World War. One terrified young woman, walking to work one morning, was paralysed with fear believing she'd become the latest victim. However, a rusty nail protruding from a wall proved to be her attacker! Whether the 'slasher' actually existed or not is shrouded in mystery.

The Woolshops

To walk down the familiar slope of Woolshops is to walk down an ancient and fascinating street. It has been said that Woolshops has changed with every generation of Halifax folk, something of an exaggeration perhaps, but, nevertheless, Woolshops is certainly one of the most altered streets in the town.

Originally a narrow, cobbled street, its overhanging buildings reminiscent of The Shambles in York, Woolshops marked the boundary of Halifax town centre for anyone entering from an easterly direction. Weavers with their laden packhorses would sell their cloth in the Piece Hall and then move on to the 'wool shops' for their new stock before returning home as they had come, via Beacon hill.

The first 'fast food' establishment in the town was probably the Royal Fish and Chip Restaurant at the top of Woolshops in 1905. By the 1920s Woolshops still contained many businesses but had a sad, worn air to its narrow sloping street and had gained a reputation as a rough part of town.

June, 1931 saw the opening of the Princes Arcade, part of a regeneration scheme for Woolshops. The Princes Arcade could be entered on Market Street, where nowadays Boots the Chemist is located, and the 'L' shaped walk through would lead the shopper to exit on Woolshops. The scheme included 24 shops, 14 of them actually in the arcade. Some early tenants were The Star 'O' Wallpaper Co. and Mr E Duce Hairdresser but the flagship business was Modelles House of Fashion serving the ladies of the town with latest styles and designs until its closure in 1979. Modelle has been replaced by WH Smith. The arcade was an attractive building with a square, tower-like structure over each entrance. A magnificent lamp standard stood on a central island at the top of Woolshops in this period and Meesons chocolate shop, at the top of Woolshops, delighted shoppers at Easter with a display which filled the window from top to bottom with chocolate eggs decorated with the names of the lucky recipients.

The 1960s saw Jeffrey's furniture shop adjacent to the entrance to the Princes Arcade and Fred Moores Electrical Appliances shop was immediately below Modelle. The Portland Galleries occupied premises each side of the entrance to the Arcade and Ryleys men's outfitters used to trade from the bottom left hand side immediately above what was Sainsbury's and is now Marks and Spencer. There was two-way traffic and large car parks at the bottom of Woolshops gave a clear view of the Parish Church.

Perhaps Woolshops' most well known building, the timbered premises at the top, is said to be the oldest building in the town and of Tudor origin. Recent renovations have included painting the timbers red, said to be the most likely original colour, rather than the traditional black we associate with Tudor buildings. Some feel that the £250,000 cost of renovation has left the building looking fake rather than authentic.

The biggest change of all came in 1983 when the present Woolshops shopping centre was officially opened. Discussions around the building of an Arndale Centre for Halifax had been going on for some time, the final outcome was Woolshops as we see it today.

The New Talbot Inn, in previous centuries the scene of cockfights where gentlemen could bet as much as 50 guineas on a result, where the first meetings to discuss the building of, what was to become, the Royal Halifax Infirmary took place, was finally pulled down. Mothercare now stands on the site.

At work

The delivery of a new boiler for Fair Lea Mill at Luddenden Foot drew a small crowd of spectators as can be seen in this photograph dating back to the 1930s. This was one of two coal fired boilers brought in by rail to provide the steam to run the mill - and clearly built by Musgraves of Bolton! The boilers were handled into the mill from the railway station, around half a mile, by a system of pulleys and chains, highly skilled work and the men certainly knew what they were doing.

Courtaulds had taken over Fair Lea Mill before its relatively recent closure and a resident of Luddenden Foot, Mr Raymond Lawless, remembers clearly celebrating his 50 years with the company in 1972. He describes it as the best weekend of his life and as he is now close to 90, it must have been some weekend!

Mr Lawless and his wife were taken from their home 'in the Foot' to Manchester by taxi. In Manchester all of those employees who had chalked up 50 years

with the company met up and boarded a coach bound for the Lake District. A stop was made for a slap-up lunch and sets of towels were presented by the company representatives. The party headed on to their posh hotel where a dance in their honour had been arranged for that Saturday night. Mrs Lawless was given chocolates and could choose from an array of corsages in various colours, appropriate flowers to wear with her dress for the dance. Mr Lawless found the bar that night and imbibed a little. Chatting with a company director who had also imbibed a little, he was told he'd be a fool if he went home without any cigarettes which were available in plentiful supply. Mr Lawless took advantage of the offer! At a wonderful dinner that same evening, the employees could choose a commemorative gift and Mr Lawless chose a silver cigarette box with £100 on top. The final day of the trip included a tour of the Lake District and more gifts and presentations.

Right: Sparkling white aprons but would a modern day Environmental Health Officer approve these premises? Sunday dinners of roast beef and Yorkshire pudding seemed to have more mouth-watering flavour in the days before refrigeration but perhaps that is no more than the effect of memory rather like the summers of one's childhood always being sunny and warm.

This photograph, believed to have been taken in the 1950s, shows a fairly typical, very well stocked butchers shop, in this case in Luddenden Foot beside the busy Burnley Road - exhaust fumes and emissions but there never seemed to be food related illnesses. It appears that a house sat on top of the shop and perhaps it is the lady of the house we can see, in clean pinafore, on the balcony. Could she be the butcher's wife? The butcher and his boys appear proud of their shop and display although the pigs' carcasses spread each side of the window seem almost obscene in these days of pre-packaged, cling-filmed and processed pork chops in the supermarket chiller. The sign in the middle of window could boast some kind of chilling system and could the items each side of the window be Christmas decorations?

Butcher's boys often delivered meat on pushbikes with a basket attached to the handlebars, the baskets often carrying a sign showing the name of the shop or proprietor. The meat arrived in neat packages, white paper on the inside and then wrapped in brown, sometimes an abbreviation of the contents and price had been scrawled onto the brown outer paper by the butcher in a thick pen.

Below: The roof on the right of this photograph is that of Fair Lea Mill at Luddenden Foot. The traction engine on the left edge of the shot is no doubt assisting in the removal of an old boiler in the days before the Second World War. Has something gone wrong or did they mean to knock the wall down?

Fair Lea Mill made products from imported cotton waste, products such as towels, sheets and cotton blankets. In the days when this photograph was taken the workers would have worn dark blue bib and brace overalls over a striped cotton collarless shirt. The narrow stripes on the work shirts were often blue and brown on a white-cream background and the cotton fabric was thick and bound in plain white around the neck. A collar could be added by using a small collar stud often made of brass. The studs were also used to fasten the shirt when a collar was not being worn and, if they were dropped, were difficult to find! The temperatures in a cotton mill had always to be kept high and constant so that many workers went barefoot in the summer. Clogs were often worn in the winter.

The chimney to the left of centre in this photograph is that of Helliwell's Textile Mill.

A good head for heights was an essential characteristic for anyone involved in the construction of mill chimneys - as this picture clearly shows. Two brave men perched high above Fairlea Mill in Luddenden Foot were an irresistable subject for J.T. Sellers when he visited the location with his camera. Textile manufacturing was central to the growth in wealth and population Calderdale experienced for at least two centuries. The industry was initially conducted in the homes of those involved in it. Later, water and then steam-powered mills sprang up and the industry became centralised in these noisy, tightly-managed environments. The advent of steam power required the building of thousands of tall mill chimneys which characterised the skyline of many West Riding towns. By the 1950s a combination of the decline of the industry, the availability of a reliable electricity supply and affordable electric motors made the use of many of them unnecessary. By the 1960s and '70s hundreds of these carefully constructed chimneys were blown up or pulled down, returning the skyline of much of the district to its original contours.

Could this be Dews Garage in the 1930s? Dews still stands at the town end of North Bridge.

The car on the left of this photograph, attracting the attention of the chap with the raincoat over his arm, is a Vauxhall 1914-18 war car and Prince Henry graces the right of this photograph. The car in the middle at the back is the 1926 Vauxhall 30/98 Tourer. The 30/98 was first listed as a standard model in 1913 although individual cars had been built for customers before then. It was guaranteed to lap Brooklands at 100 mph!

Readers may be interested to know that a new Vauxhall Cresta would have set them back £1,077 in 1960 and that included over £300 in purchase tax. A new Triumph Herald convertible, in the same year, could be yours for £766 25s 6d including purchase tax of around £225. In 1965, by which time you would need a new battery, a Duralife Standard Battery would cost £3 16s and a complete driving course, including the test, at the Ash Tree School of Motoring in Hipperholme came with a 1965 price tag of £10. Now convert all that into decimal currency!

Above: An interesting photograph here. A reminder of what must have been an exciting Saturday afternoon in the 1930s - a July 27th to be precise. The people of Halifax are being exhorted to attend - 'DON'T FAIL TO WITNESS THIS ATTEMPT' screams out from the board on the back of the truck. At 3.30 pm this truck will be fully laden and will attempt to climb Old Lane, Triangle, an extremely steep and curving road which, in those days, would be cobbled not smoothly covered with tarmac. The truck is a 30 cwt Chevrolet belonging to Trinity Garage whose name still appears on Huddersfield Road, Halifax.

Triangle village lies each side of the main road out of Sowerby Bridge leading to Ripponden, (and ultimately the M62 and Manchester), and lies in the Ryburn Valley with its very steep hillsides.

Mill Bank is an attractive old village high on the hillside above Triangle. The old cottages of Mill Bank have attracted many residents interested in renovation in recent years and geraniums flourish in window boxes and terracotta pots. The mill has been successfully and attractively converted into living accommodation as has been the fate of many mills in this area, for example in the centre of Sowerby Bridge and the luxurious apartments in the mill at Rishworth.

Right: An old Leyland wagon with solid wheels belonging to Holdsworths haulage contractors forms

the centrepiece of this photograph from the 1920s. The 'Petrol Filling Station', back left of the shot, which boasts a Rolls Royce saloon car for weddings at 'moderate charges', is located at the end of Commercial Street where the ABC cinema now stands.

IW Holdsworth Ltd celebrated their 75th anniversary of their founding on November 30th, 1948, with a staff party and ball at the Victoria Hall in Halifax. Around 450 guests were invited to join in the fun. The firm's founder, Mr Israel Holdsworth, began his business career with a horse and cart in 1873 but this, his first venture into the transport business, lost him all his savings and investment when his horse died! However, a highly successful company was eventually built and throughout the six years of the war the firm ran a nightly trunk transport service without a break through the blackouts and, sometimes, intense air raids. Miss Holdsworth, a daughter of the family, giving a speech at a dinner after the war, amused her audience by recalling that their vehicles ran on gas during the war due to petrol shortages. She said they stopped to fill-up at gas lamps!

In 1924, Holdsworths inaugurated the Hebble Bus Co. and readers may remember catching the dark red double deckers, often on the Bradford route in the 1950s, because they looked so different from the green, cream and yellow livery of their Halifax Corporation equivalents.

Below: An unfortunately familiar view of Halifax for anyone travelling in from the general direction of Bradford in the 1950s and early 1960s. The town lay like a thrown shawl sprawled over a shoulder of the Pennines, the valley filled with soot and smoke out of which poked a never ending vista of mill chimneys. The chimneys, in this shot too numerous to count, were the main contributors to the smoky smog filled atmosphere but were assisted by emissions from the railway, gasworks and houses with coal fires. A long way from the post-Clean Air Act Halifax of today!

How many readers can remember 'lighting the fire'? It wasn't always the turn of a switch and the automatic ignition of a clean, fume free gas or electric fire. In the 1950s the coal might have been kept in the cellar or in a coal bunker outside the house. A shovel and a bucket or scuttle were needed to bring the coal to the fireplace and it was often dark, cold and raining. Zippos were firelighters which came in a black box with an orangey-red flash. Firelighters, 'cakes' of easily combustible material were sometimes used to get a fire going or newspaper was folded and twisted to make the basis of a fire with firewood laid in a criss-cross on top. Newspaper was held over the fireplace to create a draught to make the fire roar into life and the coal dust seemed to get everywhere. Remember waking up in Januarys with ice on the inside of the window and then having to light the fire?

It is difficult to determine the exact spot from which the photographer took this shot but the foreground would appear to be Dean Clough and the chimney with the jagged castellated top, left of centre, looks very much like the chimney, loved by kestrels, which still stands on Old Lane and carries the date 1879. Is that the Peglers building on the skyline top right of the photograph? Also on the skyline, a little to the left, is what could be the clock tower of Crossley Heath School, formerly the Crossley and Porter Grammar School, and behind it Wainhouse Tower.

Right: Road widening on Rochdale Road in the Pye Nest area of the town. The centre of the photograph shows men working with shovels, not a pneumatic drill in sight - can that be described as a blessing? The onlooker, on the right hand side of this picture, is wearing a white muffler, or scarf, extremely popular at the time and probably made from a silky fabric. The original steps, against the wall centre left of the shot, can be seen and the steep drop is being precariously negotiated by someone moving downward, bottom left of centre. The roadway is made up of 'sets' which were a bluey-grey colour and always gleamed attractively on wet evenings in the glow from the street lamps. A set of temporary traffic lights stand towards the centre right of this photograph and how necessary they were judging traffic volumes by this picture! Trams ran in Halifax for almost thirty years and the two set of parallel tram-lines can be seen here running along the highway. The last tram in Halifax ran on St Valentines Day in n and was on the Ovenden route. Trams could take up to 100 people, including standing spaces, and it has been said that they could clear a waiting crowd very quickly.

Left: Fifty years ago, or thereabouts, if you'd worked in an office it would have looked something like this. Your job title could have been filing clerk or typist or switchboard operator or even the exalted rank of chief clerk. What is certain is that you would have had a specific role which limited the range of your duties. These days office workers tend to be multi-skilled and the receptionist also operates the switchboard, the word processor, the fax machine and the photocopier. None of these machines existed at the time this shot was taken.

Wearing a suit and tie to work was a bit of a status symbol in those days, many a parent aspired to 'a suit and tie' job for their sons and definitely an office job rather than 'going in t'mill' for their daughters. The hairstyle worn by the young woman in the centre of the shot was a popular one. An old stocking or a specially made product was pulled onto the head and then long hair was rolled around and tucked into it. These young women could have used Ponds Cold Cream and fashioned home-made shampoo out of White Windsor soap. Shampoo wasn't as readily available then as it is now and soap was sometimes shredded and melted in a pan with water for hair washing night.

Above: George Square and the construction of the building which would eventually house smart shops and be fronted by park benches and flower beds and pots. This would become a very pleasant part of the town and one where citizens still like to sit on sunny days. Irvine Lodge the well known Halifax hairdresser had stylish premises in the centre of this block and at one time, Hagenbachs confectioners traded from here.

In this photograph the placards fronting the new building are advertising Scotts Porridge Oats, Sanatogen, Guinness (is good for you), Walls Sausages, Daz, Stork (can you tell Stork from butter), and Acdo.

These were the days of headscarves, also known as 'headsquares' and sometimes worn as turbans. Metal curlers had taken over from the agonising 'curling rags' inflicted on little girls by loving mothers but the occasional singeing application of the curling tongs may have continued. Teddy Boys were arriving on the scene and girls favoured full, gathered skirts with wide elastic belts and stiff, net petticoats which made the skirts stand out. The 'New Look' from Norman Hartnell was being worn by Princess Margaret and everyone wanted to follow the trend. Pencil skirts and high heeled shoes were 'in' and the worrying, to the older generation, arrival of rock'n'roll was on the horizon.

Outskirts

Left: Six happy young women, clearly good friends, stroll down the daffodil bordered drive of White Windows, Sowerby, in the war years. Their hairstyles, typical of the period, are evidence of the date this photograph was taken, the 1940s, most likely during the war. White Windows is a Leonard Cheshire home these days. A residential and nursing home for people with physical handicaps. The home is a charity, dependant on donations for their work which includes respite care - looking after people for a couple of weeks whilst their regular carers have a holiday - as well as those who make White Windows their permanent home. The house has been extended and has large, well maintained gardens for the benefit of the residents. Apart from the girls' hairdos, this photograph can be dated to the wartime years because, in that period, the house was used as a hostel for young women brought down, mostly from the North-east, to work in the mills. Many of them stayed in this area, married and raised their families here.

What would these young women have missed in the war years? Stockings were in short supply. Sweets perhaps? Sweets were strictly rationed as were most foods. Cadbury's chocolate with one and a half glasses of milk in every bar possibly? Every citizen was rationed to 2oz of bacon and 1oz of butter per week and dried eggs, which came in a cylindrical tin, were generally the order of the day. Some people preferred dried eggs for scrambling and almost everyone adored the state orange juice but not the cod liver oil!

Above: Mytholmroyd nestling in the beautiful Calder Valley. This shot taken in post-war years and looking towards Hebden Bridge and Halifax shows Thornbers Chickens on the 'Top Land' to the right of the photograph. Thornbers at its height was the biggest poultry breeding firm in Europe and existed from the early 1930s until the 1980s. The site of Thornbers Chicks is now Orchard Park Industrial Estate but is still owned by the Thornber family.

At the back centre of the picture is the railway station and further over to the left Radcliffes Moderna mills can be seen. In the foreground of this shot Scar Bottom Mill is clearly illustrated. This has now been demolished and the Stocks Estate built in its place. Mytholmroyd Church is behind and to the left of the mill.

The distinctive lighter coloured roof in the bottom left hand corner of this photograph is thought to be Rosemount House, former home of the Thornber family, with its garden stretching out in front.

The meaning of Mytholmroyd can be determined by breaking down the word into its three components - 'Myth' means two streams joining, (in this case the Elphin and the Calder), 'holm' means a flat area surrounding a joining and 'royd' means a stony clearing. Mytholmroyd therefore is 'the flat stony clearing surrounding the junction of two streams'.

It's much easier to say Mytholmroyd - unless you are a railway announcer from the far side of Lancashire!

Left: An overall view of Mytholmroyd in the beautiful Calder Valley in the late 1930s - early 1940s. In the upper right hand corner of this photograph, a copse of trees hides Ewood Hall and the Ewood Estate was to be built around this area. Broadbents Foundry can be seen as a long low light coloured building to the right of centre. Some of this building is still there. Behind and to the left of Broadbents is the site of the Bankfield Estate, still in the future when this picture was taken. Further to the left a gasometer can be seen in the area known as Redacre which contains the beautiful Redacre House. Lower left of this shot, Stocks Road can be seen as light coloured and curving and Calder Avenue is in the foreground. Mytholmroyd is famous for its annual world championship event, first held on April 13th 1971in Hebden Bridge. The event was reported in the national press and filmed by Yorkshire Television. Preliminary heats were held in the Gas and Electricity Showrooms in Halifax where 50 competitors were whittled down to 12 finalists. Mrs Betty Horsfall of Hebden Bridge became the overall World Champion and held the coveted Courier Trophy for a year. The event? The Annual Dock Pudding World Championships! For interested readers or would-be world champions, Polygonum Bistorta Dock leaves are the best for puddings and these can be found in April. The ingredients are: 2lbs of Docks, 1/2lb of nettles, 2 large onions, 1 bunch of spring onions, 1 knob of butter, 2 tbsps of fine oatmeal, salt and pepper. And, to quote Jimmy Young's radio show, this is what you do: Boil all the ingredients together, roll the result in the oatmeal and then fry in bacon fat and serve with bacon for breakfast.

Below: Salterhebble as it once was! A dramatically changed part of Halifax. Now a thoroughfare for traffic coming from Junction 24 of the M62, the bottom of Salterhebble has been the scene of many traffic related changes designed to improve the flow - and the tempers of drivers held up in lengthy bumper to bumper queues as they travelled into Halifax! The car in the foreground of this shot is believed to be an old Austin.

The area of water seen to the right of middle in this shot, is believed to have been a dam possibly serving Naham's Mill which stood on the spot now occupied by The Quays hotel and public house, (formerly Jenny Dees). The remains of the mill's chimney can still be seen in the hotel car park.

Halifax General Hospital stands at the top of Salterhebble Hill and will become the site of Halifax's new hospital at the beginning of the next century. The attractive old lock at the bottom of the hill is still there to assist longboats negotiate the canal. Nowadays the longboats tend to be hired by tourists rather than operated by traders.

This photograph taken from the Exley end, shows the amount of demolition which has taken place in this area. The Shell garage now stands in roughly the location of the building left of centre in the shot, beyond the chimney. The Calder and Hebble public house, named after the river and the canal, fell victim to the demolition in this part of town where now traffic lights and a mini-roundabout control the traffic.

Above: Rochdale Road leading to Sowerby Bridge and the police have been called to an accident. On the left of this photograph, near to the lamp standard, can be seen the old road sign pointing motorists in the direction of Rochdale, Oldham and Manchester. Rochdale Road led over the Pennines and into Lancashire.

It's difficult to know exactly what had happened here and which of the pictured vehicles had been involved. Presumably not the police car! The British Road Services wagon, on the right of the shot, would have been painted a drab, olive green. BRS were hated by other road hauliers of the time. The old Morris to the left of the picture, at an angle to the old Humber, (the police car), would seem to be the vehicle most likely to be involved in the crash.

This section of Rochdale Road hasn't changed a great deal since this photograph was taken in the 1940s. The sets on the highway have of course been replaced with tarmac and there are no 'cats eyes' in the shot. A Halifax man, Percy Shaw, invented 'cats eyes' having hit upon the idea after following the reflection of tramlines on a foggy night in 1933. In 1935 he set up Reflecting Roadstuds in an old stable near his home in Boothtown and there began the manufacture of a product of truly global proportions. Drivers on murky evenings have good reason to thank Percy Shaw.

Right: A view of Oxford Lane, Siddal probably dating from the 1950s. This photograph was taken from the junction of Cinderhills and Oxford Lane looking towards Halifax - the 'far end' of the village as Siddal people would say.

To the right of centre of this picture can be seen Siddal Baptist Church.

The first church was built in 1859 and the chapel we can see in this shot, was built on Good Friday, 1888 - an appropriately holy day for the opening of a church.

The original stone walls still flank Oxford Lane but the buildings on the right hand side of the road in this picture are now all demolished. In their place these days are modern, brick built bungalows and new houses stretch up the hillside behind. Dr Lord's surgery is further along the right hand side of the road. The left hand side of this part of Oxford Lane is overgrown with bushes with signs of allotments and concrete footings.

Siddal came into existence between 1830-1851 and developed into an identifiable community referred to by the residents as the 'village'. The meaning of the name Siddal has defied the efforts of history boffins but it is likely to be a corruption over the centuries of a simple description, for example, in modern day parlance, 'farmhouse, 'hillside' or 'deep valley'.

Fifty members of Siddal Community Centre published a booklet in 1989 entitled 'Siddal: Our Memories, Our History' which gives an account of living and working in Siddal in the early part of this century.

Left: Do readers remember all those old Hovis advertisements on television? 'Ee when ah wer a lad ah 'ad to push t'bike up t'hill'. Northern scenes such as the one on this photograph, the old Pack Horse Road at Heptonstall, had to be the inspiration behind them. This road, still well used by walkers, was, once upon a time, the scene of a Coiners funeral and the coffin had to be carried up this road by trudging bearers. People living 'on the tops' at one time had chemical lavatories and the 'muck cart' came to empty them.

This picture, believed to date from the 1950s, shows Hebden Bridge in the background and the distinctive sight of houses built on the steep sides of the valley. To the left of this shot now stand Hebden Bridge Medical Centre.

Heptonstall is an ancient and beautiful village. Its church is dedicated to Sir Thomas a Beckett who was murdered at Canterbury in 1172. Heptonstall church is estimated to have been originally built in or around 1260 but very little of the original building remains. The church was in use until 1854. The village also attracts its fair share of tourists. In the late fifties increasing numbers of American tourists were noticed visiting the village principally on 'Methodist Heritage Tours'. Ten years later literary tourists began to arrive after the American author, Sylvia Plath was buried in Heptonstall churchyard in

the 1960s. Sylvia Plath, whose works include the Bell Jar, was married to Mytholmroyd born Poet Laureate Ted Hughes.

> *Heptonstall church is estimated to have been originally built in or around 1260 but little of the original building remains*

Above: A view of Elland in the late 1950s-early 60s when South Lane School was still standing and Kwik Save was yet to come. Most visitors have their first view of Elland from the dual carriageway coming down the Ainleys from Junction 24 on the M62. The town can be seen spreading across the valley and hillside with its new and old homes, old mills and new industrial estates. The building famous for supplying pipe-smoking Prime Minister Harold Wilson with his Gannex raincoats still rises up to meet the eye and the new BUPA hospital can be seen on the left travelling up the Ainleys towards the motorway. The building of new roads for motorway access around Elland has changed the edges of the town considerably. The old road up the Ainleys still exists and now houses several companies on a new industrial estate. The development of the Lowfields site near to the new roundabout off the motorway access road, has been the hoped for source of many jobs for the area. Lowfields is one of the few flat areas with good motorway access in the district. The familiar sight of Elland Old Bridge still greets visitors from Halifax and renovation work on buildings and land has made improvements to the appearance of the waterside.

Right: A wet and rainy evening on King Cross in the 1960s. This photograph is taken from the Pye Nest end and is looking towards Halifax. The Old King public house can be seen left of centre as a lighter coloured building with bay windows. Kennedys the Barbers was located in the block to the right of this frame in the middle of the two main roads. The road in the foreground leads onwards to Luddenden Foot and the Calder Valley.

The amount of traffic in this shot may not be heavy by the standards of today but shows a considerable increase over photographs of earlier decades featured elsewhere in this book. In local dialect this could be described as 'prooagress' and 'moor 'orse power'! To quote from a dialect column in a local newspaper,

'An' Ah'll tell thee wat, an' awl. It wer a bloomin' seet cheaper fer fowk wen they'd nooa big garage bills ter pay. At leeast, wen tha took thi 'orse ter t'blacksmith ter be shod 'e'd nooan think up another hauf-dozen jobs 'at wanted dooin' to it!'

Bottom: Many readers will recall the view of King Cross shown here as it was in the late 1960s. This is the junction with Rochdale and Burnley Roads before it was widened and flattened and filled with traffic lights and traffic lanes. Along the parade of shops, left hand side of the photograph, was Mrs Priestleys Toy Shop. Further along was Wendy's Fish and Chip shop. The Feathers, seen centre back of the photograph, still stands and Haugh Shaw Road leads off to the right. The Old King is visible on the right of this picture and somewhere around here used to be a dark blue box affair with a tap attached to provide water for the steam engines after they'd made it up Bolton Brow!

The well known Danny Gethins Pie Shop was across the road from the Old King. How many readers can remember visiting Danny's with a basket containing a pudding basin and a cloth. It was necessary to take your own container and a large pudding basin in a shopping basket provided stable carriage for the pie and peas you had to carry home. The cloth protected your supper and helped to keep it warm!